GODSPEED

Hitchhiking Home

GODSPEED

Hitchhiking Home

Laurel Lee

Harper & Row, Publishers, San Francisco

Cambridge, Hagerstown, New York, Philadelphia, Washington
London, Mexico City, São Paulo, Singapore, Sydney

FIRST EDITION

Library of Congress Cataloging-in-Publication Data

Lee, Laurel.
  Godspeed: hitchhiking home.

  1. Lee, Laurel.   2. Christian biography—United States.
3. Christian Churches.   I. Title.
BR1725.L27S3   1988   289.9 [B] 88-45143
ISBN 0-06-065223-3

---

88 89 90 91 92 RRD 10 9 8 7 6 5 4 3 2 1

Dedication

This is the author talking from the center stage of the dedication. I'm applauding. I have corsages and bouquets. Now, in alphabetical order, will you come foward and be acknowledged.

Position the spotlight on Teri and Jerry Carbone. In the office of the BIG Corporation they spun the manuscript into word-processing machines.

The Donatonis' made a home for my daughter, and the Guldseths cared for my son.

Bob Luken is both friend and brother, and I have popcorn for my sister, Pam. From Fremont into forever is Sherri C. Please rise Linda and Robert Sillins.

I want to thank you in sincerity and love. Whoever reads dedications clap with me. These people made all the difference.

Preface

The following book was compiled from a series of journals that were kept by the author in 1966 and 1967. The contents chronicle adventures, yet extend beyond to provide a glimpse into an age itself. As Laurel wrote in her early diary, "I think about us, the people of the sixties, as being like leaves. We must be autumn's generation, full of color and blowing in gusts of wind to every direction.

"The fifties, before us, were a uniform foliage holding fast by their stems to branches."

This is a journey into adulthood, that whimsically records the discovery and acquisition of universal truths.

GODSPEED

Hitchhiking Home

OREGON
June 12, 1966

I am serious about trying to get us a lift. Staring at each glass windshield I look for the face over the steering wheel. It's eyes I want, so mine can make a solemn plea; I am a human sign with a request that they please stop and yield.

It's easier to get rides when I'm alone, but Ted is with me. Seated in the roadside Queen Anne's lace, he looks to me like a kind of gentle bear with his full, dark beard contrasting with the flower caps. As he reclines on his elbow, his long hair brushes the plants. Each stem holds a cluster of white, pinpoint stars, and he is the giant in their galaxy. I envy him getting to study the constellations in the flowers, while I'm at work standing in the gravel.

In the two days that it has taken us to get out of California, it has been proved that the best configuration for us to solicit rides is him seated to the side. So my arm is the one that is cast at a permanent right angle to my body. Since I haven't smoked any marijuana yet today, I can remember to keep my arm taut and my thumb popped up. It's exactly like fishing; I am the lure.

Time, it seems, is as slow to us as the afternoon sun. Our only hour hand is the lengthening shadow.

"If we lived here, Ted, we could tell the month by the black-berry bramble. Look by the fence. It's a tiny, green knot now in June."

I see the old car as we are speculating whether the plant would still have some red leaves left to mark November. The vehicle looks like an antique Ford laboring some in its uphill

1

climb. Still glossy black, it was designed before my birth in the forties.

Becoming conscious again of my thumb, I wish it would enlarge and emit colored sparks. The driver looks to me, in this flash of passing seconds, to be in his late twenties, and without any other passenger. But his pace does not slacken.

"What's the difference between January and February with the blackberry bramble?"

While discussing its unfurling leaf in the eleventh month of May, we get our ride. I am not even trying for transportation at this point. I have even temporarily forgotten that I have an extended hand. It's a surprise to hear a truck crunch to a halt on the gravel forty feet from us. Instantly we are animated, as tenths of seconds matter now. We are athletes in the hitchhiking Olympic dash. As my sleeping bag unrolls and starts to drag along the ground I glance up at Ted and I can see him weighing whether to turn back and help me. When he stays with the truck, I feel that I'm wrestling the giant anaconda snake alone; the bulge in it is no longer my clothes but its last rodent dinner.

After finally joining the men in the cab, my ride evaluation system goes into effect. The first fact is the smell of the driver smoking. Next is the sound of his double-speaker amplification of country and western music. I observe that his hand on the wheel has a wedding band, and on the same arm is an artless tattoo. Like a kind of echo, I can feel our host making his own judgments. My long brown braids and my companion's beard have already labeled us hippies. I know that any front seat biographical information that I can offer will only underline his first deduction. I think about Ted and me while inspecting the scented cardboard pine tree that's hanging from a visor. I have just finished my junior year at Berkeley as a sociology major. Ted is from the East Coast, and our relationship has never been anything more than that of talking friends.

As my attention shifts to a Smokey the Bear litter sack hanging from a radio knob, I think about our trip. It was really Ted's idea. We had been up on the roof of my building watching the evening sun catch the panes of glass on the houses in the hills. Ted was always ready with ideas, and offered them like sticks of gum that we could chew together.

"Laurel, maybe the Eastern nations of the world matured spiritually, while the West concentrated on technological development."

I was still holding my breath so every tiny door in my lungs could open to the smoke of the joint.

Ted became increasingly animated with the thought that enlightenment is a definite experience, beyond the natural opportunity life offers for gradually expanding understanding. We had scrunched down to sit in the roof's gravel for seclusion while we smoked and were leaning our backs against a wall. After exhaling Ted would paraphrase the literature of Indian mystics. Our attention had gone from the extended panorama of Berkeley and the distant bay to the irregularly rolled cigarette between my thumb and forefinger. The idea of going to seek enlightenment came like spontaneous combustion. I threw the roach down as we began to plan a hike into some secluded woods to meditate and fast.

"It has to be a commitment," insisted Ted.

"We will not leave our place of seclusion until we are altered.

3

I read how it happened to the young Buddha as he sat under a tree. There're all kinds of accounts of out-of-body experiences."

The driver flips open the top of a cigarette pack and extends the box over our laps. Ted refuses with a few syllables, while I just shake my head. The cross exchange of destinations reveals that we are sharing his cab for only a short ride.

Getting out at the far edge of the town, I'm already calculating the best spot for cars to pull over before they accelerate to the highway speed of 65. While I adjust the cord that binds my sleeping bag, Ted begins to thumb, rather than sit, in the litter of discarded Dixie cups and gold paper that once wrapped hamburgers.

As an old automobile pulls off the road and the driver gestures for us to come, I feel I'm standing by a slot machine that's just registered three stars. There's a rumble of a coming jackpot as I identify it as the same antique Ford that I yearned for earlier.

"No more room in my trunk; one of you will have to sit with your stuff in the backseat."

I like the driver. There's a hint of a drawl to his voice, and the lines around his mouth are those of a man who's smiled a lot in the sun.

"My name is Richard."

He has on a khaki army shirt with loose threads on his upper arm where a field badge has been pulled off.

"I'm going over to the coast once I'm farther into the state," continues our driver. "I'm hoping to take a month and do some camping and fishing. I've even got lobster traps in the back."

As Ted replies that our intention is wilderness backpacking, I am feeling like a tiny jigsaw piece with the right number of protrusions and indentions to let us fit together for our passage to the woods.

Choosing the backseat, I let Ted slide into the front. Behind our driver I study the waves of his hair. He keeps it trimmed to where I can still see his neck, unlike my companion, whose brown ends are matted between his shoulders and the seat.

"I'm from Los Angeles," says Richard.

His statement half asks us for our own city of origin. His eyes catching mine in the rearview mirror make me be the one to reply.

"Ted is visiting the West from Boston; I'm a sociology major at Cal in Berkeley."

A line of additional biography comes to mind, but it never goes from thought to voice. Ted really came looking for beatnik fame. He brought a suitcase of his poems to take to Ferlinghetti, who runs the City Lights bookstore in San Francisco, but nothing ever came of his submission.

"So, you're from LA," injects Ted. He begins to tell our host of a billboard that he saw by my apartment advertising a California carrier plane with the line that "Los Angeles is now only sixty minutes away."

"The joke," says Ted, "is in the graffiti. Someone scrawled across it, 'Scary, isn't it?' "

I can tell it isn't an appropriate story. Richard, by his feigned chuckle, obviously doesn't understand the Bay Area's disdain for the state's southern city.

Leaning back on the bolster of sleeping bags, I retreat from further dialogue to watch the subtle movement of the telephone wires and to choose which roadside pine has the best shape for a Christmas tree. The men begin to look for isolated logging roads to make camp. I know it's dinner they really want. The evening light in the Northwest will have sun until after nine. Richard finally elects to turn in at one of the frequent state parks by the side of the highway.

"Hey, get a load of that line of vending boxes selling all the newspapers!" hoots Ted.

Richard laughs at the sign advertising bundles of firewood for sale. "This is how the suburbs go camping!"

I realize that we are the aliens, speaking in our dialect of ridicule. The sense expansion of the drug experience has done the separating. I doubt any of the other campers in this ten-acre facility have ever seen walls dissolve into liquid, changing colors.

"Look," I point out the number of trailers that show in their windows a small square of bluish light denoting someone watching television.

With one mind we choose the most distant camping site, veiled by rhododendron bushes. Richard begins to unload his gear, while Ted goes and sits on top of a picnic table.

I pull out both sleeping bags, feeling irritated at my companion. His head is bent reading that one set of initials loves another set of initials. I slam his bag down next to him, but not even the zipper registers a click.

"Look, Laurel," says Ted, "I can see in the history of this campsite a fervor of high-school patriotism and these declarations of love." He begins to fish between the flannel sheets of his sleeping bag looking for his notebook. He wants to write. I leave him, feeling the obligation for one of us to go help Richard, who is beginning to gather firewood. I can feel my low-level resentment that Ted gets to be the artist while I'm cast in the role of patron. I have my own brand-new diary that I would like to work on.

"Look especially for pinecones, Laurel. They make good tinder."

Looking over at Richard, I'm fascinated by this man stripping a tree of dead limbs and snapping them to a uniform length. He is so vigorous compared with Ted.

"Why are you really taking a month on the coast? I don't think anyone from Los Angeles can possibly relax that long."

He flashes a conspiratorial smile. "Seeds," he replies.

His teeth appear to be refrigerator white with the slightest gap between the two in front. It's his tan face that accentuates the brightness of the enamel.

"I have mayonnaise jars full of marijuana seeds, and my plan is to cultivate a small plot that I can come back and harvest later. It's become the cash crop of the year. The serious underground farmer is working out of rural greenhouses."

Unbidden, Bob Dylan's new chorus comes to mind. My memory even has the full accompaniment of his scratchy band:

They'll stone ya when you're trying to be so good,
They'll stone ya a-like they said they would.
Everybody must get stoned . . .

I find a nest of pinecones and follow Richard back to the camp fire pit. I feel sad that morning will bring our passage to the sea, and separation. Lives seem so much like cords that can braid together for a moment, then immediately unravel. Nothing seems permanent.

After depositing my load of tinder, I stare at Ted, who is still hunched with his book. Flicking a pen, he seems to be counting the syllables to some invisible meter.

"That lad is sad, a cad, and bad," I hiss at him, but not really loud enough to be acknowledged. Turning to the woods again, I decide to look for flowers with enough stem to pluck for our table.

June 13

There are three things I'm watching. Mostly Ted's back. Ever since we left Richard near noon and started our climb, I've been following the square of his rumpled shirt. He has his sleeping bag draped around his shoulders the way some peasant women wear their shawls. I keep looking down at my shoes too. The rubber rim of my tennis shoe protected my foot from the dripping grass for only a few steps. Then, the dark water blotching began. I know my socks will be penetrated; I'll soon be marching for enlightenment with wet feet.

I've also been looking back at the sea. It is going to disappear, as our path is about to dip among fir trees. Because of the over-

cast sky it is hard to separate, in my quick glances, the distant gray line of the ocean from the air.

I wonder about Ted. I'm curious about whether he is hum-ming some sacred Sanskrit syllable with a mind that is becom-ing like blank walls. For all I know he may already be in the land of one hand clapping. Or, is he like me? I'm on the verge of clamoring for a full plate or a hot bath.

"Hey, Ted, let's stop a minute." I haven't used my right to call a rest yet.

Saying nothing, he turns back to me. I wish for a friendly, "Oh sure," or "Good idea," but he is surprisingly mute.

"It's too bad there's no sun today." Still, he says nothing. I try again: "How long do you think we'll be here?"

"That's just the point, Laurel. It's time itself you must come to release." His voice has a pedantic edge, like that of a professor about to lecture. His very tone dashes my hopes that we can turn around and look for Richard, to see if he has set up his lobster traps.

I now see the pursuit of enlightenment to be like the best ten-nis game. He is making me feel that now that we have come all the way to Wimbledon, I want to leave the court and go find fish and chips. Ted, by contrast, is obviously pressing the strings on his racket.

A hawk previously frozen on a limb lifts to the side of us into the air. Never seeming to beat its wings, it only sways on some upward draft in its ascent.

"Now, look at that," says Ted.

I know to him it's a symbol, but to me, it's a bird. I feel discouraged that he is the poet again, and I'm gathering wood. He's obviously destined to experience the throbbing of the galaxies while I'm left cleaning the mud off my feet with a stick. As Ted adjusts his bag and pivots from me, I feel self-loathing. The "hate me" chorus is gathering again in my mind. I don't feel ready for some religious experience, yet I'm not honest enough to publicly admit it and turn around. I walk accused, listening to each of my irregularities. I can even hear my parents' voices haranguing me about my life-style, which provides constant heartache for them.

The vista of ocean is gone. The fir trees are dripping from branch to branch, and all the bushes are glistening with a permanent dew. We begin to march through a ravine of squat skunk cabbages. To avoid the mire I try to step on the vegetation itself, leaving behind me a trail of crushed plants. I think of it as creating evidence that a bigfoot creature does live in the mountains of the Northwest. The whole idea of me eight feet tall and covered with fur makes me wish for some marijuana. Some ideas lend themselves to a smoking exploration.

"Do we have any of our stash left, Ted?"

This time my trail leader pulls off his sleeping bag and wads it up on a rock. Instead of fishing between its folds as I expect, he leans against it and faces me. Somehow a piece of moss has lodged within his beard. I stare at the incongruity of the green spot instead of focusing on his eyes.

"Why do I need to remind you of our agreement? Look, Laurel. It's no drugs or food, and we stay here until we blast through all these things that our flesh is always demanding. I don't think a lot of talking is good for us, either."

Out of a multitude of rebuttals and protests, a single sigh is barely audible. I feel utterly dismayed that I even got myself into this. Last night he was glad to light one joint after another until we were acting like three of the seven dwarfs, Dopey, Happy, and Sleepy. It will soon be getting dark, and I'm not even sure that I can find my own way back.

"As for our camp," Ted continues, "we'll just know the right place."

His presumption makes me feel I should yell at him. Maybe the combination of exertion and emotion would make me warmer. Instead, I remain still.

Ted surprises me by not resuming the lead. He begins to walk beside me. This small physical gesture has power. I feel somewhat comforted. Yet it doesn't prevent my continuing images of dampness. I now resemble the kitchen sponge that has absorbed old water on the drain board.

"Are you sure, Ted, that Buddha sat under one tree until he experienced enlightenment? Hypothermia has about the same amount of syllables."

"Let's stop for the night at that ridge," he replies, ignoring my jab.

Following his motioning arm I see a spot on the top of a hill that appears to have scrub bushes instead of trees. Most of the day we have wound ourselves through woods dense with trunks. It is a mountainside that has never been harvested for its value in board feet. Knowing I can soon stop makes me like the horse that sees the barn. I don't even feel winded and edge ahead to take the lead.

At the top my socks have to be peeled off; I put the sodden mass of them on a bush. Once in the flannel sheets, I begin to be warm. Yet, one satisfied need seems to make what is unsatisfied roar. I am starving. It feels like empty spoons beating out a tattoo in my stomach.

"I want you to know, Ted, that I am dying and all the significant meals of my life are now passing before my eyes." I can tell by his sharp sideways glance that he feels sarcastic humor has no place in the path to higher consciousness.

"Do you want to quit, Laurel?" Rolling onto his side in his sleeping bag, he faces me. Tones of voice can sometimes seem louder than what is uttered. I am surprised at the lack of judgment in his question. Stilled by his unexpected acceptance, I affirm that I do want a life with a spiritual dimension.

"But this trip, Ted, purposely depriving ourselves of food and probably sleep, is not going to open any permanent revelation for me."

In his silence is a terrible moment of not feeling I belong anywhere. I can't live in suburbs and measure curtains, or in universities worrying about tenure and publishing in journals that nobody reads. And now I know I can't practice any significant self-denial, which is what produces mystics.

"I'll help you find that LA guy's campsite in the morning, if that's what you want."

Even as he speaks all that I can envision is Richard Lee's food locker. I despise myself that appetite is such a prime motivator.

"Laurel, all that I left in Berkeley was a small suitcase of poetry. I've decided to go east, and someday I'll write and tell you where to forward it."

I feel neither sad nor surprised. It just seems to be the way of things.

Once it is dark, my dreams are as tissue paper too frail to keep me wrapped in any real sleep. There are no stars to ponder, but mercifully, no rain either. Ted snores and my legs ache from being so tightly curled up to my torso. Feeling imprisoned by so many contradictions in myself, I think about the melancholy music of the slaves, "Sometimes I feel like a motherless child," and other lyrics that sing of separation.

June 14

Opening my eyes to morning I see real shadows and not the solid, drab earth from yesterday's overcast. The surprise of a blue sky brings to mind an American ditty once sung in my first classroom. I utter it out loud with feeling.

And out came the sun and dried up all the rain
And the itsy, bitsy spider went up the spout again.

Ted is already awake hunched over his notebook of poems.

"Do you want to hear mine now?"

The truth is I don't want to hear it, and never do. I'll be polite again. Today I feel I should because he's leaving, while all the other times it was because I had just met him.

> Time
> It moves
> Texture to patterned texture
> Staccato quarter tone to texture
> Predetermined involution
> Last to first. Last to last . . .

Trying not to make any noise, I wring out my socks, counting the drops while Ted continues. Years of a talking mother have skilled me to fold my mind away from ears that hear.

Once on the trail it's my lead. I only have to go downhill and look for the ocean. The water will become the compass point. Seeing our tracks through the ravine, it is obvious that in crossing the belt of skunk cabbages three times, we were making lopsided circles in its bordering woods.

Down on the road where we climbed out of the old Ford, I yearn for movie bloodhounds. I want dogs that can track tires and old exhaust vapors to Richard's camp. Ted makes a few suggestions, but his mind has really moved east. It's almost as if he's talking to himself of café haunts and old friends.

The fact that Richard has to have automobile access to his camp is my best clue, and his statement that he would be staying close by. I make a rule that for my first searching hour I will refuse to shout and call his name. Even in starvation I need dignity. Finally, I spot a colored tarp through the trees, a blue plastic sheet that looks like a kind of rectangular kite too big to rise higher than its post between the trunks.

Our host is absent, which allows me to stare openly at the range of his supplies. He has real sheets and blankets on a cot.

The lantern and stove, fish hooks and knives are laid out with drafting sheet preciseness. I feel like a third-world country staring at an industrial nation.

It is Ted who strides to the wooden food cupboard. I watch him tear open a package of crackers and thrust two into his mouth. His act frees me of any fingers of guilt that I am keeping him from some sacred destiny. I take delight in every crumb lodged in his beard.

We both can hear the whistling of Richard coming. It's not a song, but a jolly noise that turns to a laugh as he spots us.

"Wasn't it just yesterday morning that I dropped you off?"

"Now," replies Ted, brushing at the cracker bits on his chin, "experiences alone can create a kind of time zone. A day to a traveler can subjectively be a week long."

"Did you ever catch a lobster?" I know I asked the wrong question as Richard starts laughing his protest that he hasn't had enough time. Ignoring his mirth, I begin to explain our new plans.

"Tomorrow, as Ted goes east, I'll probably start hitchhiking back to the Bay Area. I rent in Berkeley only during the school year, so for the summer I can stay with friends in the Haight."

Richard looks at me. "Between yesterday afternoon and today, I've really finished what I needed to do. I'll be glad to drop you off in the Haight-Ashbury."

I know he has planted every secret seed from his mayonnaise jars. Nodding back, I feel flattered that on my account he is willing to abandon the oversight of his garden to the summer's chance rainfall and sun.

June 15

There's a kind of luxury in looking out at hitchhikers from the Ford's front seat knowing I won't have to stand at any curb except the one at my destination. I like Richard too. He is ready to talk and listen in equal amounts. I choose what to emphasize about myself in the sharing of both dreams and history. We come together as wet clay, and I mold for him my features with my words. Instinctively I seem to know the fragment of him that matches something within myself. With Richard Lee I disclose my streak of rebellion.

"So in high school I had a prank a week. My style wasn't the common things like sneaking cigarettes or flipping a match in the wastepaper basket, but real plots to undermine the school powers."

My hands are flying in front of me while I speak as if they found an air pocket without gravity. I try to tether them to my lap and continue to describe Washington High's room 1, which had a wall of pigeonholes where the faculty collected their mail. Since the teaching staff was large, I was able to mount my own name in an empty space without detection.

"Receiving every announcement, I learned they were removing J. D. Salinger's books from the library. Other policies that I felt needed to be exposed were brought to my attention. So, with one friend, I used the mimeograph machines to make a secret newspaper. My distribution system was to push a copy through every locker vent."

I look at him. Telling a story needs some response, so I can gauge the size of the canvas to paint it on. Richard's "so what happened" breath lets me explain how I was caught on Valentine's Day.

"I had sabotaged the new typing teacher by signing her name to the cheapest possible cards and forging a statement that she was new at the school and hoping to make friends. But the joke was that I didn't give them to everyone.

"I was cracking up as I watched the teachers' surprise at finding such a greeting card, then others sorting through their mail with wry expectation but finding nothing. My hysterics roused the suspicion of the dean."

From the corner of my eye I can see Richard turn his head from the highway to briefly look at me.

"You know, I'm seven years older than you, Laurel."

My response is the internal, simple addition for the sum of twenty-seven.

"But when I went to high school in LA—the San Fernando Valley—I remember dodging the police."

As he explains what about the specific styling of his car attracted the attention of squad cars, I study him again. There's a definite fineness to his bones from the wrists on the steering wheel to a slight tracing of facial cheekbones. His shirt is the same khaki army issue of the other day, but it has the fresh precision lines that mark a laundry.

"I knew alleys," he continues, "and as soon as I saw the distinctive markings of a squad car, I would slip on a golf cap and hunch down in my seat to imitate an old man trying his son's vehicle. My time was never so important that, upon identifying a cop, I couldn't go in the opposite direction.

"As for me, Laurel, I finally just quit school and then immediately took a high school equivalency test."

Looking over at Richard, I'm stunned. I have never met anyone who purposely withdrew from high school. Between nursery rhymes and baby cereal, I, and all my friends, were told that some day we would go to college. It was the C that followed A and B.

"Why?"

"It had nothing to do with what I really wanted. I wanted to see the country and learn the things that aren't in textbooks. Knowledge isn't necessarily wisdom. I worked a lot of odd jobs around the States."

As he tells about stints on Montana wheat ranches and experiences riding the rails, I begin to think how he resembles Thoreau, who wanted to go and live deliberately. My thought seems to unfasten a small internal chamber of admiration. I can compare Richard to Melville too, who wrote that whaling ships were his Harvard and his Yale.

"My parents," continues Richard, "both had problems with alcohol. When they divorced I lived in foster homes until my father remarried and brought me and my younger brother to the Valley."

I can feel that Richard Lee's thumbprint history has all the markings of early hardship.

"You know, Richard, I really wanted to get my master's degree and be a social worker. But last year I was part of a summer intern project in Chicago tutoring grammar school dropouts."

I loved the children, but changed my mind on public service as a career after seeing how caseworkers are paper-chained to their desks.

"I know exactly what I'm going to do." His voice is more announcement than statement. It rings with all the certainty that my own tone now lacks.

"I want to homestead in Alaska. Look, Laurel, the land is free, and it won't always be that way. You can stake out a minimum of five acres, or up to a hundred and twenty."

As he begins to list the qualifications, I look out at the scenery of the Pacific Northwest. I try to dissolve the fast-food restaurants and housing tracts to imagine its first raw magnificence.

"The house has to meet specific dimensions, and the applicant also has to be resident in it for a given number of months each year. If a homesteader claims more than five acres, then a percentage of the property has to be cultivated."

As Richard's words describe the necessary labor of the frontier, I think of moose herds and salmon schools. There could be Eskimos that throw one into the sky from a circular frame, taut with skins. There are dogsleds for racing across fields of snow.

17

"Richard, think of the marijuana you could grow in the summers under the midnight sun. You would be the only supplier of "Caribou Gold," or "Midnight Madness." Listen to this: "A Klondike stash is better than hash!"

"Do you want to come to Alaska with me?"

"Sure," I reply. We have to use the lightest of tones so we can retreat into pretending it was only a joke, if necessary. I think about us. Our conversation seems to be like a long braid of hair. The talk of homesteading has become its one decoration, and now the old strands begin to cross each other again in the established pattern of sharing his times with mine.

"I do love to travel, Richard. Once I even posed as a phony South Sea island princess, trying to obtain free passage on a Hawaiian cruise ship."

He wants to know all about it, and I explain that four years ago, at sixteen, I wrote to Matson shipping lines and inquired if they would exchange a free trip for me generating newspaper publicity for their company.

"Instead of saying no, the typed reply inquired what promotional ideas I had in mind. Having been influenced by 'I Love Lucy,' I decided on my first plan. I wrote the society editors of San Francisco's two papers and Oakland's *Tribune* and announced the arrival of the princess of Neureteka. She, I explained in my imitation press release, was coming to negotiate with Matson Lines for their South Sea ships to stop at her father's island.

"My thought was that they would put a small filler in the paper mentioning Matson Lines, which I could clip and submit, but instead they all requested interviews.

"My parents were not cooperative. They took a dim view of my losing a day of school to go to the city coated in makeup. When I tried to reschedule the interview to a Fremont restaurant parking lot, the *Chronicle* and *Examiner* declined, but Oakland sent both a reporter and a photographer.

"Feigning an accent, I gave my perceptions of America, which were to become a Sunday feature story. I compared rock 'n' roll to our own village traditions of music. Unfortunately, the week before publication, a car hit a telephone pole outside Washington High, knocking out all the electricity. The same reporter assigned to Alameda County news came to cover the story and found me in the hall. He was furious, and I ended up back with the dean of students."

"At least you've never been in jail," laughs Richard.

I look back at him, but somehow am hesitant to ask more. He seems like a brew, with something dark and intoxicating about his person. In the suburbs there were only Boy Scouts who grow up to be doctors and lawyers. Here is my first real Indian chief.

It has been so pleasant talking to Richard that the day has dissolved far too quickly. I'm surprised when I notice that we're just north of the Bay Area.

"We're going to be in San Francisco soon. Now, just where do you stay there?" asks Richard.

Looking out my window, I can see the hills covered with round oil refinery tanks. I explain about the commune in the Haight. It's a typical narrow house having common exterior walls with the other clapboard residences along the street.

"With the exception of some upstairs bedrooms, everything is open to the company individually allowed by the permanent residents. We just roll out the sleeping bags anywhere and put donations in a kitchen can.

"It can be weird. I heard one man yelling once because a chicken was boiled in the pot he uses only for rice. He kept saying his food was going to be ruined by animal vibrations. Yet there is generally a spirit of a new kind of extended family that shares and practices tolerance."

"I couldn't stay there," replies Richard. "I would hate the disorder of it, and because of drugs, it would be too risky with city police always doing some bust."

"No," I retort. "I think that risk is for the dealers' houses. The narcotics squad isn't interested in our little stashes, just the source and distributor of kilos."

It seems like a tiny argument, a miniature X in our dialogue where my opinion crosses his.

The freeway, I notice, now has a new lane for each direction to accommodate urban traffic. Before us is the steady, red stream of taillights matched by an equal flow of white headlights. Except for the emerging dark hole marking the bay, all the rolling land surface is illuminated by electricity. Streetlights, lamps in homes, and commercial neon coat the earth.

"We do garbage sculptures there." I point out at the dark land strip between the freeway and the bay.

"Just using the debris that washes on the shore, we only need wire, hammer, and nails to build things. There've been windmills and old locomotives, but I ache now to pound out a reindeer." It was the creation of antlers that I could envision, with intricate wood-scrap horns.

The bridge, Richard comments, is designed so that vehicles approaching San Francisco have the top tier with a panoramic view. Little can be seen from the bottom lane that's leaving the city.

"I'm just going to drop you off, Laurel, and drive on. I'll be careful to get a copy of the address and write. It's important that we get together."

I mumble something short and affirmative, not knowing if he really means it or not. Intention is like a suit of clothes. It can look good on the hanger of a promise, but I wonder if this one will ever be worn.

THE HAIGHT-ASHBURY
June 29

There is really no entrance hall to the commune, just a space to come in and shut the door before climbing the immediate staircase or turning in to the living room. A rock 'n' roll poster for a Family Dog concert has been thumbtacked to the wall. Sometimes the fact it's crooked bothers me, but never enough to un-pin it and make it right.

I look down at the house mail; there is nothing again from Richard. It has been two weeks, and I despise my subjective cal-endar that marks the time without news from him.

Walking into the living room, I sit on the couch and survey the table in front of me, which is an old ship hatch door coated with thick varnish. The daylight exposes blobs of hardened can-dle wax along with the dust and ashes, plus the ends of incense sticks, that litter its surface. Someone has brought down a cou-ple of kitchen chairs from upstairs, and across from me is a giant blue water bottle stuffed with an arrangement of weeds.

I feel I need some marijuana to turn the dark sedan of my thoughts into an open convertible. I know I have to do some-thing other than attend the night's ongoing party. It's Alaska I want. I feel possessed by every travel poster or reel that has ever showed me Mount McKinley and Alaska's uninhabited forests.

Thinking of options, I remember I can go to Yosemite and work another summer for Camp Curry. That was my plan when

I first gave notice to the manager of my Berkeley apartment. Yet this address in the Haight-Ashbury is my only possibility for connecting with Richard. There is no house resident responsi-ble enough to forward a letter.

Impatiently, I kick out a foot and retract it. The floor has some large soiled pillows on the green rug along with all the instrument cases and bedrolls.

I have to get up and walk. The impulse to move seems as strong as evolution. Some fish refused to stay in the water and had to crawl up on land. I don't want to be a giant sea slug like the rest of the house residents. They sleep until noon, then eat peanut butter out of jar with a spoon.

Out on the porch I'm glad the air is cool enough for my long-sleeved turtleneck as I start down the street. The only ones not striding by are a kid selling joints and a bongo player swaying with his drum on some stairs.

I decide to browse the shop windows. The record company has almost hidden its albums within piles of what must be minced oregano. Next door the dress shop has emptied its display windows of mannequins and put in their place a line of folding chairs open to the public. One couple, looking like Wild West Indians, has come to sit and watch the pedestrians. In the wake of heavy construction to install underground pipes, deposits of silt have sifted up the curb and across the sidewalk. Two men have plopped deck chairs in the sand. They are reclining in swimming trunks with iced drinks.

My depression is only temporarily diverted by the sights. It feels to me like a wet garment that can be unbuttoned but never taken off. Even in the middle of cities there still should be some rocks left for kicking. Golden Gate Park occurs to me as a source of small stones; I'm glad for even the smallest destination. Feeling sick of myself, I prescribe a quick spoonful of trees.

Trying not to stop now, my intentions weaken at the Wild Colors paraphernalia shop's display of roach clips. This is the tool that came of age with me, created for holding the burning butt of a joint so all the marijuana can be inhaled. Beside kiln pottery and Navajo peace pipes are sterling silver flatware. Welded into the place of fork tines is a tiny mechanical claw.

The park is one shoreline of the Haight-Ashbury. Beyond the curb are waves of trails and trees. I have a favorite place. Strolling along hedges, I veer off the path near the first children's playground. There's a spot surrounded by bushes and trees where I can lie prostrate and feel invisible. The grass is long and wild, having escaped the scrutiny, and the shears, of city gardeners. I pluck and tie grass blades around my fingers. It's the knots that I identify with. I feel of like fragile substance and equally tangled. Stretched out in the sun I'm glad it's too late in the day for dew. Even though the day is cloudless, I know a line of fog is most likely lurking out on the ocean.

As I roll over on my back men and relationships are on my mind. There was only one I ever hoped would propose marriage. Bob was a Berkeley teaching assistant who got his master's degree analyzing the original illustrations in *Alice in Wonderland*. I even sewed four extra pockets into the lining of his coat, as he was working on numerous journals and wanted them all at hand.

I remember one of Bob's favorite books was on dolphins, and we came here to Golden Gate Park one night planning to climb the aquarium wall and swim with them in the open tank. Since I was wearing the wrong shoes I couldn't scale the decorative relief on the building as he could. Bob whispered down from the top that he would wait another night for immersion—only he got a grant and left immediately to go to Spain and write about the art in *Don Quixote*. I had thought my days to be like a fluid that could have been contained in the cup of his plans, but he never asked or wrote for me to join him.

Reaching up my shirt, I extract a joint from the natural pocket in my bra between my breasts. I wonder what percentage of women fall in love with the life-style that a man offers. Expelling the smoke, I exert my will to try and blot out the dream of Alaska. As other women look to pour themselves into silver-rimmed goblets, I had wanted a hand-hewn mug of the last frontier.

Using my fingernail, I begin to shred the grass, seeing how many strips I can cut on each blade. It seems clear to me that neither Richard nor any other man can bring to my life the bloom of fulfillment. I am really my own gardener. Yet I feel I lack the tools. Is it time, or something else, I need to exchange these rubber utensils within myself for something that won't bend with every pressure?

Sitting up, I decide to go to my parent's house to wash everything, then proceed to Yosemite's employment office. Maybe I just need work. Plans prop me up; I always sag inside when I don't know what to do.

On Ashbury I see what I think is a Vietnam protest group. One man is holding up an enlarged cartoon of President Lyndon Johnson riding a bull in the sky that is dropping excrement down on America. The sign next to it reads, "Where is Lee Harvey Oswald now that we need him?"

The bongo player is still there but now flanked by both a guitarist sucking a harmonica and a man with a congo drum. Their look and beat is "happy drugland."

In the house I can hear kitchen sounds upstairs: water and talk, the radio and pans. As a financially noncontributing guest, I have tried to live on the edges of this home's life. I straighten things and do not argue with obvious absurdities. It's my opinion that constructing a pyramid above one's bed does not imbue those that sleep beneath it with more power, and other odd theories.

Now, anxious to depart, I push my belongings from behind the couch into my sleeping bag. I'll hitch across the bridge to the Nimitz Freeway and down to Fremont. Leaving this neighborhood for my parents' is like climbing off a train of gypsy wagons for a house in the monotone suburbs.

My mother always has dinner ready at 5:15. Every night there's a green salad slicked with Miracle Whip. In the seventeen years I lived at home I never saw them run out of toilet paper or laundry detergent.

Once up the stairs, I survey the kitchen from the doorway. While people turn gray with age, linoleum and sinks turn yellow. The tenants have tried to decorate with posters of French cafés and the scrolled philosophy of "Desiderata." John stands with his back toward me frying last night's rice. Melissa is drinking tea in her short kimono, and Rob is spreading peanut butter on health food store bread. They all seem suspended in separate bubbles.

"I'm leaving for the Sierra," I state while thanking them.

Melissa writes my parents' address on the wall by the telephone. There's an eighteen-inch circumference of phone numbers, including the free medical clinic and local legal defense organizations.

John puts down his spatula and takes an envelope off the refrigerator from the middle of a stack of *Berkeley Barb* newspapers.

"I think this came for you some days ago." It's a telegram with a Los Angeles postmark. I read: *"Come. In the light. Need you. The earth."*

After Richard Lee's name is an apartment address in Venice, California. Knowing Richard, I feel the cryptic, mystic content is part satire. It's safer when you invite someone to live with you to make it sound a little like a joke.

Instantly jubilant, I feel wise. In giving up, I received. By walking away, I arrived. I wonder if it's a law of the universe, or if I'm being just as silly as those who believe in the power of a pyramid above their beds.

VENICE, CALIFORNIA

July 1

Richard's not in. No one answers my knock. I stand in the hall with my gear knowing he's the type to lock his door even before I try the knob.

I've unfolded the telegram so many times that it's starting to feel like parchment. Number 15 Dudley Court is at the end of the first floor of a small apartment house. I can see a flash of sand and distant water reflections about a block down the street.

Leaning against the wall, I slide down to sit on my bag. I really want a bath. Maybe, I speculate, as more people "turn on" and "drop out" television ads will be created to market products to a nation of hippies. A sunny day of hitchhiking could be the backdrop for selling any kind of organic soap or beauty product.

SHIP OF DOUBTS

I want Richard to come. I wish for a book for my waiting. Doubts are beginning to float through my mind in ships with black sails. My thoughts are now full of pirates who are plundering my excitement. Closing my eyes, I let my images sink into the mud floor of my dull tiredness. The day had too many dashes to vehicles on highway shoulders and one-dimensional conversations. Exhaustion covers me with their silt, too deaf and blind to watch for anyone.

I sleep until my shoulder is being shaken as a voice repeats my name. Richard is holding a fishing pole with a tackle box at his feet. It doesn't matter that cars are clogging eight full lanes of freeway and the skyline is gray with exhaust; this man looks as if he has just strolled out of Oregon's woods. Since it is visible that he's glad for my presence, the terror dissolves that he would arrive with women at each arm announcing that the Alaska helpmate job is filled.

As the door swings in I can see the kitchen. It looks to me like a facility born and raised in a trailer before being retired for service by the Dudley Court apartments. The bathroom is on one side. I stare at the tub, declaring my devotion to running water. The living room is furnished with a regulation couch and table, but the hi-fi belongs to Richard. The bed, I'm told, is behind these double doors that he taps while speaking and has to be lowered at night to the floor.

"You can have it," I declare. "The couch looks fine for me."

A million things, both visible and invisible, can be communicated in the most polite and simple of sentences.

The room aches for art. This time I'm carrying some small beauties. In my pack is a prized tin candlestick and some illustrations of passages in *Moby Dick*. I plan in the morning to glean some flowers from a yard and look for seashells to put on windowsills.

We eat chicken. Richard went to buy it as I bathed. My wet hair hangs almost to the plate. I can't pull it back, because my hands are slick with Colonel Sanders's eight-spiced grease.

"Tell me about your experiences with LSD."

The question is posed to me in a quieter voice than Richard has been using.

"Both of us, you know, Laurel, have been ahead of our times, as even today it is still legal. We were among the first."

It occurs to me that the fuse of its legality must be short and burning through the court system into a law against possession.

"My initial experience with any kind of drug, Richard, was with LSD."

I was thrown out of a conservative private college in Oregon for hitchhiking and waited in Portland to complete my transfer to Berkeley. There, I became friends with artists from the museum school, who invited me on an acid trip.

There was more planning than impulse. We had a meeting beforehand that included organizing both food and music. One man, Joe, elected to remain straight and oversee us. I felt we were getting ready for outer space. We were a crew of four flying to the stars by swallowing a pill called Owsley's "white lightning."

I sat on a sleeping bag on the floor as my reality altered. It progressed from an initial heightening of hues to watching every surface in the room, and even the air itself, undulate with intricate patterns of colors.

"The strongest sensation was that I had been like this before. Maybe it was an illusion that rode on the back of the hallucinations, but I felt convinced that my earliest infancy also had a shimmering view between the bars of my crib.

"My thoughts had the speed of a river with too much racing along the beds of my mind, between words, to actually communicate. Speech came later when we took our old forms back in the old room."

"With me," interrupts Richard, "there was the same expansion of senses. It was as if I could feel the pause between the notes of a symphony. But my central experience came in looking out a window at an El Dorado Cadillac parked by a curb. It seemed fancier than the rest of the cars because, I realized, the driver had to show his worth in things."

Richard was quiet. I could feel his search for words. Some ideas float higher than language or pictures.

"The car started me considering houses, clothes, and all the accoutrements of civilization. I felt I understood for the first time a part of the meaning, and extent, of vanity."

I interrupt, "Both of our drug experiences were like being elevated above earth's parade for a few moments, and now we'll never fit back into formation, or execute the right steps."

"Laurel, I want a quality of life that's defined by something other than things or talents."

"Alaska," I whisper back. "Okay. When do we go?"

My statement is so quick it acts like a pin that pierces our great balloons of philosophy.

"Money," he replies. "My plan is to build a miniature log cabin on the back of a flatbed truck. It could be designed with a loft for a mattress, and a tank could provide gravity-fed water to a sink below. I'll have to find a small wood stove."

"Could you build bookcases?"

"Sure," chuckles Richard, "but only for paperbacks—hardcovers would add too much weight."

We're now thoroughly intoxicated with future visions, and our conversation dwindles to separate thoughts. With my fork I'm beginning to draw stars on my plate when Richard suggests a walk.

The sidewalk may as well tilt toward the sea as we cannot go any direction but toward the water. I think about how much I like this man walking next to me. His motivation seems like an arrow straight in flight to the north. So many of my hippie friends have become so blurred with drugs that they cannot even lift themselves to the height of having a goal.

Looking up at his profile, I consider offering what feels like the ultimate sacrifice. I could get a job, although my preference is to read good science fiction in bed. Waitressing does provide daily tips, a free meal, plus a minimum-wage paycheck. I have to consider whether I'm really willing to spend eight hours a day taking orders for pork chops and filling catsup bottles.

"Richard, getting a restaurant job is a lot like hitchhiking. I just step into the slow-moving vehicle of a café and make words like an extended thumb asking for employment."

"Great," he replies. "We'll start tomorrow, and there're so many gas stations in Southern California that I can easily get hired. I bet there's a day coming when they are going to make customers pump their own."

Wryly, I reflect on his enthusiasm for me to work.

"Maybe I should give one week to canning peaches that could see us through our first winter."

Richard just laughs in the hearty way that opens his mouth.

"We'll start here, but go next to Seattle or Portland for buying the truck and building the cabin."

There's a wide sidewalk through the sand bordered by palm trees and an occasional refuse can. Some retired couples sit on benches. Their voices punctuate the sounds of the surf. I imagine they are talking of deeds long done, while ours are before us. I take Richard's arm as my salute to the arc of life.

July 16

I'm sure it is just sweat, but my grim imagination makes me feel that my perspiration is part grease. My forehead is damp, and the first swell of each cheek under my eyes itches with moisture.

I hate my job. I'm now standing by a small service window pushing out hamburgers that I cook on the grill behind me. With Richard needing the Ford, I had only the radius in which I could walk to look for work. There were no real restaurants with air-conditioning and padded booths that needed help, so now I live by day at Herb's fast food.

Marking an order for french fries and shakes, I reach over to the machines that I'm supposed to clean at the end of my stint. My employer is a middle-aged man whose chest fell, ounce to pound, into the waist of his pants. It's not his bulk that offends me, but the feeling that the subject most dear to him is nude women. When he's behind the counter, Herb takes orders looking square into a customer's bosom instead of her eyes. With resolve I grip my rag and wipe the counter; my impulse to heave it at him is almost overpowering.

Never have I watched a clock like the one mounted above the sandwich buns. At 10:00 A.M. the hands make an open jail cell. The white apron that I don is as good as handcuffs. My sentence is seven hours of hard labor. Now, it is four. My feet ache, and Herb is looking through a girlie magazine in the closet turned into a kind of office.

"Hey, Laurie. Start cleaning out the shake machine."

I can see Herb rise while giving me my instructions.

Obediently, I open the spigots and let a stream of chocolate and vanilla chug into two-gallon cartons.

"Why do you always leave here in such a hurry? You know we could get to know each other."

I'm glad my back is to him. My immediate grimace would show how I despise what's below the surface of his sentence.

"Can't, Herb!"

"You got a boyfriend, huh? You know there would be plenty of advantages for you, Laurie, if you'd just loosen up."

I turn to stare at Herb. My glare takes him in, from his receding hairline down to his black-and-white-checked polyester pants hanging over crepe-soled shoes. I know with certainty it's my last day.

Feeling a little afraid of him because he's both stupid and big, I search for words that are final but won't create rage. Somehow I consider all the past girls that have had to stand here by him. Their torment must be part of the vapor in the air.

"Let's just finish this day," I state firmly.

The sight of him shuffling back to his office, more pathetic than menacing, releases the humor. I could have demanded forty free hamburgers for one kiss.

I sign the time card almost lighthearted that I will never touch it again. Usually when I see the sky, I mourn all the hours lost under neon panels. Tonight is different. I'm more infused with that ancient feeling of walking away from school to begin an endless summer.

Richard's work always begins an hour before mine, but both of our jobs end at five. I walk along the water thinking how we have each maneuvered white rags in our employment. While mine brushed away sandwich crumbs, his wiped off dipsticks and windshields. I always thought of their working motions as flags we were waving at each other. But now I've hoisted mine in surrender; I will not go back.

Fishing for the key in my drab green book bag, I begin to consider dinner. Depending on traffic, I have fifteen minutes alone at home. I put rice in a pot, chicken in the oven.

Richard eats, while I pick. Telling about my day, I can see an interest that slows his uplifting fork. Richard's attention increases. The word "quit" brings his fork back to his plate holding an untouched morsel.

Richard's eyes gaze steadily back into mine while I look for the germ of disagreement. Instead it's approval that I find.

"Great, I'm resigning too. I'll never have to listen again to Frenchie, the other attendant, extoll the wonders of Grace Kelly."

I heard about this man painting her initials all over the doors of his car.

"Why wait, Laurel? Let's collect what's due and move north. We have enough for gas, and we could work there for the truck and lumber."

The force of his spontaneity makes me feel there isn't time to clear the table before departure. A part of me, nurtured by my accountant father, considers the impracticality of leaving while there are still two more weeks of paid housing.

Yet I laugh, and as his voice joins mine I consider for the first time that I'm beginning to really love this man. He is so determined to reach his goals. Looking at him I realize character is destiny.

"Okay, Laurel, we should probably visit both our parents en route, because we won't be coming south again."

I know his family lives somewhere in Los Angeles, while mine are seven hours north.

Richard describes for me the Lee family's wall-to-wall white carpeting and orange brocade sofa. In return I tell him that my parents' family room has a machine-made braided rug and a Naugahyde couch.

"Our home," he declares, "will have a hewn-log bench layered in fur skins."

I ask in return about my kitchen while reaching over to touch his hand. I know we are beginning to speak again in our language of the future. The pending drive to either Oregon or Washington is only going to increase our fluency.

PORTLAND
July 22

I look over at the Portland skyline from a Corbett Highway turnoff above the city. It feels good to step away from the Ford; my legs are numb from inactivity. Richard puts his arm around me as we continue our low-level argument. He wants to get married. I don't think it is necessary.

"Really, Richard, what's a piece of paper?" I know I'm repeating myself. Disagreements are so dull; we keep rephrasing our own side as if some new synonym will win the other to our position.

The Willamette River below us divides the cluster of city center buildings from the distant suburbs. I watch the blocks of raw logs, bound by chains, being herded by boats under four distinct styles of bridge architecture. There's a surrounding vista of hills covered with fir trees and to the north and east, one distinct snow-capped mountain.

We can't go any farther than Oregon. Our money is too low to even consider Seattle. Upon entering the state we learned that we could glean change by picking up roadside soda bottles that we could cash in at grocery stores. I know there are some bills folded in the back of Richard's wallet allocated for renting our housing, yet he spent a portion of our checks on marijuana before we left Venice.

"Hey, Laurel, our parents will want to give us a wedding gift, and we'll request a check that we can immediately invest in getting to Alaska."

"No," I reply. "Both the Lees and the Moores think we're crazy trying to go to a land where common spit crackles into ice before it hits the ground."

"You're looking at the wrong point," objects Richard. "I think both our parents would view marriage as a rescue wagon of respectability. See," he laughs, "I'll keep you from spending another year dealing acid caps in Berkeley."

What I can't explain to Richard, as I turn from him to look at the elongated clouds, is my romanticism. Some part of me wants a request for my hand to be uttered in daisy fields with grazing horses nearby. Instead, there are highway fumes being baked in the summer heat as cars rush by us.

I refuse to say yes while a harried mother pulls in next to us so her four-year-old son can urinate in a clump of bushes. So I keep murmuring my other old phrases about not wanting to exchange vows in front of some civil servant who will be smirking at us.

Richard's voice is all exasperation.

"I don't get it. We both love each other and want the same things."

Seeing the woman look around at us while hoisting up her son's shorts, I turn back to the car. I am whispering now.

"If there's love, then let there be a wedding like poetry. Invite a thousand birds to a beach at dawn. Cut the wedding cake into the size of beaks so the wind can feed it to the guests."

Richard laughs as he walks to his side of the car. He understands motors, which are incomprehensible to me, while I understand magic. Yet our mutual respect is a strong, binding cord.

As the highway abruptly dips down, Richard discloses that we only have fifty dollars left. His voice is sober. The reality of the imminent search for both housing and work makes me feel like a balloon rapidly losing its helium. I suggest, in return, that we'd better invest first in the local newspaper to check the want ads.

As Richard double-parks, I run into a corner tobacco shop and pick up the *Oregonian* from a stack next to the San Francisco and LA papers. I feel poor. There's no such thing as uncounted change for a candy bar.

I find the car has been pulled ahead to a fifteen-minute parking meter with an abandoned nickel's worth of time. Richard scans the classified ads for employment, while I read the columns for housing. Anything under fifty dollars sounds like a flop hotel with peeling walls.

Answering my expression of dismay, Richard declares he could pawn his large drum that he fetched from his parents' house and also volunteers my typewriter that I packed from our visit with my folks. Instinctively, I guess he's resorted to these tactics before.

"We'll see," is all the speech I can muster. His suggestion creates in me an image from American history. I think of women in conestoga wagons hearing for the first time that certain prized pieces were going to have to be abandoned on the trail.

As the meter's arrow disappears and the red violation tag rises, we pull out looking for what Richard informs me will probably be a block of pawn shops. Again, I silently contrast him to the men I've known up to now, who were familiar with the process of cataloging books but never the procedure of hocking goods.

Finding what was predicted about two streets from the river, I choose to remain outside. Every possible kind of jewelry and guitar is crammed into the dusty front display window.

I find I can't wait without having to lecture what quivers within me. Real goals, I state to myself, require real sacrifice. I want to see the release of my Smith Corona to a junk shop as something noble and not tawdry: losing my typewriter feels like severing the last link between me and my university life.

Richard emerges with so few dollars compared to the real cost of our goods that I feel angry.

"You can buy it back," he explains, sounding slightly exasperated at my exclamations.

Having circled rental possibilities, we learn from a gas station attendant that they all lie in the north and southeast neighborhoods across the river.

The seeking of addresses feels like the creation of a tapestry on the city's frame. We weave between the neighborhoods not knowing when the work will be done.

I spot a For Rent sign that has not been listed in the paper. It's a small home with a porch between two white columns. A handwritten note in the front window leads me to a second house in the backyard. An old lady answers my knock. She has more scalp than hair, and a bosom that blossoms below the darts on her dress.

I realize that her age must make me look to her like a child still in braids on the other side of the screen door. So with my name I tell her that the rental in front is perfect for us, as a newly married couple. The idea of a bride causes the landlady, a Mrs. Spicklemire, to reveal she has more gums than teeth. With her now holding the key, I follow triumphant to our new back door.

The kitchen alone is as big as half the Venice apartment, with stairs in the far corner to a basement level. A table in the dining room is so old that its oak top must have held a half century of meals. There's a built-in china cabinet and chairs for company.

I call Richard in from the living room door. My thrill in the antique furniture momentarily ceases as Mrs. Spicklemire heartily declares that "this must be the groom!"

I can read Richard's eyes. The glint, with his nod, acknowledges that he has won. I will marry him. Having separately paraphrased our vows to a German landlady, she pronounces to us the words, "So you are a new husband and wife!"

There's no lease or last-month's payment required. Oregon people seem to trust more than Californians. I watch Richard count the bills, which include my Smith Corona currency, into Mrs. Spicklemire's hands. We get, in return, two keys on one ring.

Once alone, I listen to Richard, while running my hand over the black-and-brown velvet paisley on the arm of the couch. His voice swells with the grand intention to use tomorrow to track a job.

"Check through these ads, Laurel, for yourself."

I make no motion for the paper that Richard has already brought in. I know it will come soon enough. For now I'm sucking on the thought that I've agreed to be a wife in what is now a real house. Looking at the rectangle of sun by my feet on the carpet, I know I would bolt if it weren't for the more challenging destiny of wilderness. Life for me has to hold more than setting a table a billion times with aging hands. Now, it has become a compulsion to give myself to something more than arranging pleasant rooms.

August 25

The street with all the used cars is eighty-two blocks from the Willamette River. No one can even guess anymore if it were once meadow or forest. Long covered by cement, only a few weeds straggle between the cracks as witness of the original earth.

I'm following Richard down another row of trucks. He in turn is following Hal, whose name is also suspended between utility poles among plastic discs that are supposed to twirl in the wind. I'm lagging behind in the monotony of looking for the right truck. As I've heard it explained to numbers of salesmen, it has to have a big enough bed to hold the weight of the cabin Richard is proposing to construct. We have spent our last few weekends in like pursuit. Since it always seemed too permanent to see our name engraved on checks, Richard has been carrying our growing cash in his wallet for that moment of purchase.

"Want to drive this one out?"

I can see dealer Hal slap the fender of a green Ford truck.

"It's not strong enough," replies Richard. "I'm building something bigger than a camper."

I've caught up with them and have heard the elements of this conversation already this morning with "Honest" Joe and "Make a Deal" Sam.

"I've got something better in the back."

Now, side by side, we follow the salesman. My patience is like an unraveling garment. Richard can instinctively tell when I'm losing the threads of my composure. He won't look at me. Deprived of the brush of eye contact that would let me complain, I survey the cars we are passing. Most of the models are from the early sixties and late fifties. The styling of some prompts animal nicknames like "swan" for uplifting back fins, or "siamese cat" when there's a narrow line of molding over a Chevy's headlights. As I look for another rock to kick at a tire, Richard takes my arm.

"Look," he says with a voice of hushed respect. Hal is standing by an enormous truck. It's orange with real running boards and bug-eye headlights. I can see that the back frame has two tires for maximum suspension on each side.

"A 1940 International, and they don't build them like this anymore."

We need no salesman's pitch. Even with my eyes, devoid of aptitude for machinery, I can see it's perfect. The motor hardly coughs before starting. Watching Richard try it on the city street, I can see the cab tower above the common car.

After trading our Ford and counting out the required money, I find that stepping into the front seat is like climbing a ladder. As we drive I'm blind to stoplights and car lots, and deaf to small conversation. I can only envision a cabin in the snow that is high and lifted up among the mountain peaks.

"How much longer, Richard, before we can quit work and actually go north?"

I listen as he describes the layers of construction necessary to make a winter-proof house. He finally condenses the required labors into a cube of two months. Instantly I translate his estimate into the word "October."

Turning from him to look out the window, I mark the number of small shops that make up the neighborhood. They all seem like lemonade stands that adults have built on the curb. I know I would rather live under a bridge with my goods in a grocery cart than to lose the hours of my life helping customers. I think about our Monday through Friday schedule and the enforced routines of employment. Only the weekend has the breadth for some musing on philosophy.

I consider our on-the-job stealing. As an employee of Import Warehouse, I've watched the marking of goods. The price tag is triple the store's original purchasing cost for basket and bauble. Their profit level seems to justify my petty thievery. Being poor, I take from the rich.

When hired to write the advertising copy and hand-letter store signs, I took the liberty of creating my own office on the furniture floor by rearranging chairs and desks. There, my crimes take place. Committed for Alaska, I've slipped hundreds of candles into my purse. Two raw wool sweaters have been smuggled out the door with chocolate bars and other things I deem necessary for the winter. There's always a terror in my heart and every pulse point beats at the thought of being caught at the front doorway. I have one friend and accomplice, Karen. Only about eighteen, she brings things up to me while not on duty at the cash register.

Richard has brought home his own contraband from the ice cream cone factory where he works. Now, with his bags of flour and sugar, we store some of our confiscated goods in the front bedroom.

"Look, there." Richard's voice brings me back to reality. He gestures to the sidewalk. A hippie couple are strolling arm in arm. The woman resembles my friend Karen I've just been thinking about. With her unfettered yellow hair and long skirt she could appear in a sunflower seed ad. Three small dogs trot behind them. Together, we agree it's someone else.

"Richard, we're in the right neighborhood to drop in and see my old friend Triple. Let's show him our truck."

He is one of my old artist friends that I met while living in Oregon before I transferred down to Berkeley.

Triple's gray house is at the end of a dead-end street. It's covered with bleached, curved shingles, the image of fish scales. His mailbox is wired to a plow that's tied to a tree. It reads, "Ludwig Caminita III, Inventor, Sculptor, Humorist, Singer of Ballads, Teller of tales." The phrase "Bah Humbug" concludes his resumé in a slightly larger script. To us, his profession is largely dope dealing.

The porch, like the yard, is littered. It's a transient neighborhood, and Triple gleans for himself every deserted treasure. A barbershop chair is next to a number of odd-sized crates. The bell for requesting entrance dangles overhead at the bottom of a mobile of driftwood.

Stepping ahead of Richard, I follow Triple into his darkened hallway thinking how much I've always liked him. He may deviate in appearance in every possible way from the scrub-faced business man, but I feel that with Triple it's more a joke than rebellion. He's a short man, with hair that hangs in a frizzled mass of curls to his shoulders. Triple's glasses are perfectly round, in a design possibly borrowed from the owl. The smaller O's of a gold hoop decorates each earlobe. Unable to grow a real beard, he allows a few corkscrew whiskers to darken his chin.

As we are lead to kitchen chairs around an open back door, I know guests in winter must be taken to seats by the front room wood stove. Fresh air or heat mark his seasons of hospitality, while a joint is constant refreshment.

As the men begin to talk "truck" with the fluency of their species, I look at walls. A number of antler specimens are nailed above the sink so their tips can hold cooking vessels and cups. The skirt of a red square-dance dress is tacked around the ceiling light in a way that lets the garment hang down filled with air.

"We are going to get married first," declares Richard, after condensing the plan for homesteading.

"Will you trust me to craft your rings?"

Nodding back to Triple, I realize I never thought about the jewelry to mark a bonding. Knowing his whimsy, I suggest they be mechanically constructed like Swiss knives.

"I want one chamber to hold a squirting device so we can have short water fights. Then make a pop-up truce flag with the staff about the size of a toothpick."

While I take my turn sucking and holding in the smoke of a reefer, Richard suggests another compartment that could hold a small tool.

"No," I choke. "The point is a wedding ring can only have items that are related to a relationship, not any solitary mechanical functions."

With my perception heightened by the narcotic, I can see he has missed the point entirely, while Triple hasn't stopped listing duo devices. Staring at my future husband, I reflect again that his capabilities are great, but they rarely include the abstract. I have to continually bring images back to earth for him with common nouns. Having made myself uncomfortable with my own analysis of him, I sit in a brooding silence. I'm feeling that I'm not being loyal to Richard, and I've cracked open a door to some doubts.

"And then," says Triple, "I'll put a magnet in one and metallic ore in the other band so if your hands are swinging in proximity, they will automatically lock together."

As if it were a cue, Richard reaches over to envelop my hand between his. My palm and fingers lie without a flicker of life within his grasp.

I think about a carnival exhibit. Richard Lee, from a line of suitors, swings down the sledge hammer, and immediately the power of his blow can be measured. I've rewritten the degrees to be qualities of strength. It is his love for me and his commitment to our vision that rings the bell. Squeezing his hand in return, I know there are things other than conversing together with the infinite patterns of birds in flight. Women marry more than the man; they commit also to a way of life.

"Surely you can find an old church for your vows, instead of the lifeless office of a justice of the peace," suggests Triple.

"That's her job," replies Richard.

The artist resident within Triple sharpens something within me. I immediately want old wood and stained glass to surround me when I make the biggest of promises.

October 3

I'm standing outside a church staring at a sermon title mounted on a board with portable type. A locked glass door keeps the pending Sunday message safe from pranksters. My opinion is that vandals might bring improvement. I can't believe the words; they sound like the rites of savages. The pastor should probably put a bone through his nose instead of buttoning on his white clerical collar.

I have taken the afternoon off from Import Warehouse to look for a small chapel. I have already bought construction paper to hand-letter the fact of my passage from "Laurel Moore" to "Laurel Lee." Now, I need only an address and a date. Portland has a number of established churches along a street divided by a strip of park, and I am just starting my search.

It is worse in the vestibule. A bulletin board spells out, "Unless they drink of His blood and eat of His flesh, they will have no life in themselves." I wonder if I have stumbled into an obscure cult of Northwest cannibals.

Hearing a typewriter, I follow its steady tapping sound down the hall to a church office. The secretary, turning from her machine, appears very ordinary. I imagine her polyester dress covers the garishly bright tattoos, from her collarbone down to her thighs, that would be appropriate to acts of such a religion.

"Do you have a small wedding chapel here?" I ask, feeling uncomfortable.

"Yes, but it's only for members of this church. Maybe you would like to meet one of our assistant pastors. We have a large, modern kitchen that could be used for a reception."

Backing out her door, I politely refuse any further interaction. I just want to walk again on the first of the fallen leaves and see the boughs of trees covered with the colors of chrysanthemums.

The next church is soundly locked, and the exterior board asks "If God Is Dead" above the posted times of service. It makes me wonder why they even bother to go to the meetings. It seems sad to me, as I walk away, that habits could be so strong that people would sit in pews to hear the pontification of doubts.

Walking by apartment buildings, I look up and see formations of birds winging south. None of them are in the traditional V wedge but move about making their own letters of migration.

I wish for Richard; I want to talk about the sky as the only true cathedral. I've been arguing with him that we should really have our wedding outside. His reply is always a probability statement for rain in Portland. We are already a check-and-balance couple, a congress and senate vetoing each other's bills of frolic and logic.

The third church is locked too. It is a massive stone building with windows that make me wish that I could see them from the inside while the afternoon light heightens every color. The message board states, "Special Collection Sunday." The smaller print concedes that one of the needs is for new carpeting as this is one of Portland's most distinguished historical buildings.

Instantly it seems so obvious that Western religious institutions were created by the people who needed a business or who found themselves on the bank of dying and were afraid.

Seeing one last spire, I veer across side streets to reach its door. The Presbyterian church is open, and I'm ushered into Pastor John Merton's office. Seeing the number of books, I know he has an appetite for ideas—or else he dresses his walls for a scholarly effect.

After taking an upholstered chair, I blurt within my explanation of what I'm looking for that "I have to be married this month!"

As the minister replies that there are other alternatives, like counseling or adoption, I realize he has interpreted some of my words to think my urgent motivation is pregnancy.

"No," I cry, "it's the truck that is far along, not me. The framing studs are going into wall boards."

Our conversation is so knotted that I have to start at the beginning. Pastor Merton, opening an appointment book, accommodates my request by agreeing to an October 29 evening marriage ceremony, less than a month from now. He hands me the slip with this date written on top of a mimeographed form detailing Presbyterian church weddings.

With my duty done, I begin retracing my way to the park strip. I pass a small market that has put the first of the season's pumpkins in an open crate by its door. I'm sure their appearance has followed earlier buckets of summer flowers and, in turn, will be replaced by fir wreaths and holly.

Crossing the street, I take a bench and wish for a performance of squirrels, but there are only sparrows in sight. Before putting my book bag at my feet, I take out the church information papers. At the bottom, in a band of capital letters, it forbids the throwing of rice in any part of the ceremony. The rest pertains to the acquisition of the marriage license, the reception, and fees.

Last week my goal had been choosing the right colors of art paper for my announcement. Finally, I picked a light blue that is the hue of the winter sky and the shade of green like the first of spring grass. Folded in half, the covers are already complete in my best calligraphy:

Lightly balancing on the edges of time, like dew on the tip of the leaf.

A man interrupts my thoughts as he begins, in front of me, to meticulously search through the paper in a trash barrel. I can hear the voice of an elderly woman speaking in an artificial, exaggerated voice to a child.

Standing up, I start for the best street pattern for hitchhiking home. I'll have only eight days left of being twenty before my marriage. My youth has always seemed like an extended hallway lined with the doors of all my possibilities for career or relationship. Now, I have chosen to walk under one of the portals and seal myself in the room for being a homesteader's wife.

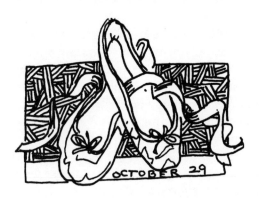

October 29

Seeing the drizzling rain from the porch, I stop to button up my coat. Richard, already in his one suit, laughs at my bundling. Since he's finding mirth in almost everything, I suspect its a form of premarriage jitters. My parents are in town for the ceremony, but we've declined a ride with them in order to walk to the church.

I have my dress under my arm in a box. It was financed by my mother as my twenty-first birthday gift, a practical, white wool A-line. Summer weather allows better for the fantasy of trailing antique lace.

The exterior of the truck is finished. It looms behind us in the driveway. Now, with the roof shingled, only the interior needs refining.

While avoiding a puddle in a sidewalk depression, I take Richard's arm. One line of a Beatles song reverberates in my mind. My brain is like a radio station that keeps repeating the same words.

"I'm Lucy in the sky with diamonds, . . .
The girl with Kaleidoscope eyes . . .

Richard turns in the wind to try and light again a fat, caterpillar-like joint of marijuana. I need some butterfly wings to unfurl in my mind.

"Think, Laurel, we're on our way to something we will never forget."

I'm now laughing as easily as he is. It does seem that experiences are usually registered as memorable during or after the event. But tonight we know beforehand.

It's cold on the Hawthorne Bridge. Only Portland's oldest black-girded structure has a design that lets pedestrians safely cross the Willamette. The reflected lights of the city vibrate below us in patterns imposed by both wind and river currents. The undulations of silver-white streetlights and office neon in the water seem like a school of animated tropical fish. I forget everything while watching reflections of red and green traffic signals appear and disappear near to the shore.

As Richard pulls me, I remember that in two hours my parents are going to watch us sing our chorus of ceremonial "I do's." Sobered, I quicken the pace.

I keep looking over at Richard in the last blocks. He's wearing a navy surplus coat that has the simple relief drawing of an anchor etched into every button. Everything in the universe feels safe. All stories with happy endings are being read aloud right now.

Once through the church doors at 1200 Adler Street we find we are alone. Richard locates the light panel and experiments with the buttons until he illuminates the small chapel scheduled for our 8:00 P.M. ceremony. Looking into the vestibule, I don't feel we belong here. The ceilings are designed with an immense expanse above a human head. It looks to me unearthly, like a habitation for giants. There's room for the creature to carry a small tree for a wedding bouquet.

Richard wants me to come down the aisle and sit next to him while he plays free-form jazz on the organ. Shaking my head in refusal, I know I can't. I have to be alone. Part of it is my continual realization that this pending act of marriage is going to be much more meaningful than I anticipated. It isn't anymore a dull legal requirement with mandatory participation, but seems like something bigger.

Going into the women's bathroom, I shake out my dress and unfold from tissue the blue Italian brooch that's to be pinned just below my neckline. With my shoes, I take out an unopened package of white nylons, doubting if I'll ever wear anything on my legs again but cotton, corduroy, or denim.

Once dressed, I study my face in the mirror. Carefully I part my hair down the middle and brush the two equal sides until every tangle has been subdued. I have no makeup, but I still pinch some color into my cheeks and use a finger to smooth my eyebrows.

I know no friends will be here. Karen told me at work she couldn't come, and Triple is out of town. Most likely my parents, alone, will be our witnesses. Richard has asked a worker from the ice cream cone factory to act as best man, but he has to be paid with half a lid of grass.

Sitting on an overstuffed chair, I can hear Richard's music. The notes rise and fall in elaborate repetition. I pretend that it's a typewriter keyboard that somehow has been converted to create music. With twenty-six possible notes Richard is composing a love letter in sound. In my fancy, I adapt for him Elizabeth Browning's lines that neither height nor depth will separate our bond.

I surmise that Pastor Merton has arrived when I hear the music stop in the midst of a rising chord. I come out to find him in an impeccable dark suit that I guess is his uniform for conducting both weddings and funerals.

"Okay, you two." I'm glad the minister is smiling.

"You didn't want a rehearsal, and am I right that you are not having any bridal attendants?"

Seeing my head nodding in agreement, he continues to instruct us to walk together down the aisle at the scheduled 8:00.

"No organ accompaniment, either. Is that right?"

Richard and I exchange one of those looks that I think means we are always hearing music.

Pastor Merton leads us into his office to wait, then later I can hear his voice sending my parents into the chapel.

Sitting together, we are wordlessly waiting for the minute hand. I wish we could invoke a blessing on our future. My feeling is for prayer, but I don't know how. I wouldn't even mind natives in body paint encircling us with voices that chant about my womb and all the gardens and hunts to come.

"What are you thinking?" I ask Richard.

I really want to ask what his meditation has been for the whole evening. But I won't risk a question that has any chance of yielding a less than rosy answer. It's too close to eight.

"Nothing. Oh, I'm wondering what all other men about to become husbands were thinking. You know, Laurel, we might have a problem in the ceremony because Triple was never able to get those rings finished in time."

Even as he is talking, I can see the bowl of paperclips on Merton's desk. My movement to reach for them communicates my intention to Richard. With dexterity he straightens the wire, then patterns it around our fingers creating the emblems of our pledge.

Once the rings are completed and pocketed, we stand and start our march. My arm interlocks with his. We have no witnesses until we appear and start down the aisle of the chapel itself. As anticipated, the room is empty except for my family and one guest. Mr. Horns, my first college art professor, must have driven down from Forest Grove on the strength of my announcement. I stare ahead. A cross above an ornate altar is the solitary decoration. To me it's a symbol that our two lives now intersect. It somehow feels inevitable, me standing beside this man to be married.

I was always the girl in the process of becoming a woman, and the future will hold me as a woman with a girl lurking within. Tonight, I feel, is the balancing of the two states.

Pastor Merton studies us. He steps down from his place of officiation, as the audience titters, to invert our positions. We didn't know that there was a prescribed side for bride and groom. Richard is now standing by his hired best man. Yet, the mood is cast. I have to push my tongue against my molars, for a moment, to keep from laughing aloud. We are the clowns up in front in polka-dot rags and red-bulb noses.

I'm surprised as the pastor begins to talk in sermonic homilies. I thought this was only to be an exchange of vows. I compare him to an airplane pilot who's waxing loquacious on the loudspeaker system. With words, he's flying us over the state of marriage and explaining how couples can keep their altitude. I paraphrase his speech to fit my image: "Only stay buckled with seat belts next to each other."

His subject now is humor and its necessity. As he explains that "God also created things for us to laugh about," I'm shot into another imaginary corridor. I envision funny beasts, like toucans with hilarious beaks, standing as a wedding pair. We are

December 1, 1966. Laurel and Richard pose outside of their nearly completed transportable cabin. Photo by Dr. S. Prince.

A front view of the truck before Laurel and Richard set out for homesteading in Alaska.

uary 23, 1967. Laurel and Richard in a familiar dside pose near Fremont, California as they mb for rides to the Mexican border. Photo by es Moore.

City Couple Lugging Home to Quiet Alasl

—News Tribune staff photo by Bob Rudsit

MR. AND MRS. RICHARD LEE HEADING FOR THE COUNTRY

Alaska Homesteaders Taking House With Them

By AL GIBBS

Richard and Laura Lee having a hard time getting from people.

They've tried in Calif Oregon and Washington s and haven't been able to "the country," Lee said. they're bound for Alaska truck which carries their on wheels.

"We're both w r i t e r s, said. "We're also both city ple but we found we h get away from the distrac We wanted to settle in O but the state's growing too

Homesteaders

"About four months ag decided to go to Alaska homestead."

Lee, 27, has built a tiny on the back of the couple's It will serve as a home he builds a more perm dwelling on their Alaska

They'll carry provisions year, Lee said, and as sc they've earned enough for a ferry ticket they'll for Alaska from Bellingha

"We're going to settle where down south around ard," Lee said. "I'm not for that Arctic Circle stuf

Future Planned

In Alaska, they'll build a substantial house, put in den, fish and hunt for their and, of course, write.

"I w r i t e children's Richard works with theo Mrs. Lee said. She ha some books published bu husband is just starting said.

Lee grew up in the Los les area. He attended Mrs. Lee, 21, is from San cisco and attended the U sity of California at Berke

Their home, at least t rarily, is tiny but efficien ganized. It has a stove, a table and book cases and a age area. The b e d r o o more storage area is in th under the rafters.

Cities Out

"When you have spent time in the country and moved back to the city realize you just can't live th Lee said. "The transition one to the other is a big ject for writing."

Besides the provisions Lees will also take along ollection of books " weighs more than the foo lot of writing paper and a puppy the couple has n a Noah.

Some things they won't though.

"We've got no clock or dar and no plans for the tant future," Lee said. " just going."

January 16, 1966. The Tacoma, Washington newspaper account of the day Laurel and Richard unknowingly chose a vacant parking lot for a campsite.

February 24, 1967. The Lees shortly after they join the House of Rainbows household.

Laurel illustrates her first book, *Walking through the Fire,* published in 1977. Photo by Bob Ellis.

Laurel Lee. 1980. Photo by
Thomas Victor

Laurel reads to her three children: from left. Anna 8, Matthew, 10, and
Mary Elisabeth, 4, in early 1980. Photo by Bob Sisson.

two baboons of the species created with outrageous rose-and-violet bottoms.

Richard's friend suddenly jerks forward and back as if he's about to fall, but catches himself. The pastor's eyes dart in his direction. With a few more sentences, Merton stitches his sermon closed. Opening a book, he asks first who gives this woman away. My father responds, "Her mother and I," from the first-row pew.

The question and familiar voice make me instantly nostalgic. "Thank you," is my meditation for paying all those Brownie Scout dues and for ballet and violin lessons. I appreciate every good word, gift, and time. It was part of your bow that has shot this daughter like an arrow, and I'm landing first, here, at this target.

Richard and I now repeat high faithfulness eye deep into eye.

Merton is obviously surprised as Richard lays the paperclip rings in his palm upon request. But the phrase "With this ring, I now you wed" has no less resonance than if we had platinum bands and sparkling stones.

We turn as "Mr." and "Mrs." The best man immediately goes and sits on the closest pew. Richard, too, looks rather pale and feeble. During our walk down the aisle, he begins to pull me over to rest with him on a seat just past the halfway point to the door. Watching him stumble over his own feet and knowing he's always been exceptionally agile makes me remember the warning that men can change as soon as you marry them.

"I really could have fainted," he whispers. "But the one fear that kept me at attention was that we might have to repeat all this again. We shouldn't have smoked so much dope."

He's barely finished the disclosure when my parents and Mr. Horns come with well-wishing words. We rise belonging to our company.

Once alone in our house, after I replace my dress with a robe, the night begins to feel more like any other. While Richard is still changing, I stand in the light of a table lamp. At my hand are two greeting cards. One is of paper stiff enough to stand; the other lies flat, constructed from a thin, lacy parchment. Both our parents have chosen a message from the Hallmark racks of wedding bell art. My parents signed "An Irish Blessing." It makes a request in the simplest of verse:

> *Now that you have joined your hands to wed*
> *May the Lord, Himself, touch the road ahead.*

December 1

"Oh, take it," says Richard. "Mrs. Spicklemire doesn't even know it's there."

It is barely dawn. I am standing on the driveway by our house. Around me are boxes of possessions I'm to hand up to Richard on the back of the truck. In my arms is a small brown rug that we had found rolled in the basement.

Late last night in bed, we decided not to spend the money for December's rent but to move into our cabin. Richard estimates that he'll have about one more month of finishing carpentry work before we can actually launch north.

"Why don't you let me climb up there to arrange things while you do some of this lifting?"

"Let's get the mattress first." Richard drops down beside me. He's wearing his daily uniform of Levi's, turtleneck, and army surplus jacket. I follow him back through the kitchen door and down to the basement. We are both nervous that old Mrs. Spicklemire is going to catch us. No one ever uses this bed that's propped against the wall under the stairs. We are leaving the springs and frame and taking only the mattress for our loft. It feels to me like a gray act, balanced between the white zone of an outright gift and the black of stealing what is used and loved. Both of us glance over at our landlady's house while maneuvering the bulk into the truck. The tag is even up that threatens legal action for removing its factory certificate. While I balance it,

Richard climbs up to the door to pull it through. I look once more at Mrs. Spicklemire's venetian blinds. We haven't told her that we are leaving, but I put a brief thank you note in her mailbox. I wish I could think of a plausible lie to pad it. She won't believe we're veterinarians unexpectedly summoned by the game department to Alaska.

Once the mattress has been concealed from view, my pulse regains a normal speed. Maybe the American Heart Association should add stealing to its list of things to avoid.

Richard jumps back down to boost me up. I'm not as agile as my husband in ascending to our doorway. I wish for fold-out stairs.

Even in the far limits of disorder, our cabin shows artistic craftsmanship. The smell is the essence of fresh-cut lumber. A diminutive wood stove is ready to be installed by a wood counter over storage shelves that still need doors. The dimensions of the handmade table are balanced to the width of the window that it rests under. There are no bookcases yet, and the textbooks and novels that my parents brought me lie in cartons. Richard is pushing still more boxes through the door, which I can only pull back into a line. I can remember how I bragged about carrying all that I needed in a sack between my shoulder blades. I am now encumbered with things, and will need to separate a box of donations for a thrift store later.

Once our goods are installed, I get in the cab with Richard. Our plan is to go to Triple's and live at his curb for however long it will take to perfect our interior. I have a kind of vacation feeling that comes from setting ourselves loose from the tyranny of clocks and calendars. Only in my diary will I try and remember to notch the dates on the page.

We are earlier than traffic. Only a few long-distance trucks pass us, some with their headlights still on. Off the road most of the houses are dark except for an occasional bulb that I imagine is for a kitchen or bathroom.

We park at Triple's but know not to go to the door. His schedule is tipped so far into the night that 11:00 A.M. is his morning.

The yard seems swamped with even more junk. A couple of tombstones that I never noticed before are leaning against the house.

With us both in the back, I can see our house has the dimensions of a tree fort. It's the first time we have both been actively moving about in the room; until now, we stood still to admire each stage of its evolution. It feels like an Alice in Wonderland-sized room, but I don't know if it has shrunk or we have grown.

"Lots of this stuff is going, Laurel!"

I'm instantly defensive. His voice is that of a top sergeant. I alone want the privilege of putting my thumb up or down over the objects in the cartons. The bulk of it is from my mother, who filled the station wagon with my old things for their drive north to witness our wedding. I can already see the set of Tupperware Jello molds that I'll never use. Even the angel food cake pan is too bulky to haul north.

"You have too many books! How many boxes are there? I would dump them all."

"Never!"

I'm adamant that the books are the last to go. We stand glare to glare.

"The idea, Richard, of being held captive by snowy elements in a solitary room without the diversion of literature is unthinkable."

My retort is like a double-edged blade. The fact is one side, but my multisyllable expression of it is the other. I know what I'm doing; I'm pulling rank to win. I went to college and he didn't, so I'll talk like a living thesis if it gives me an edge in getting my way. This awareness of myself brings a feeling of shame that I'm being haughty and manipulative. In a subdued tone I ask if we can find a compromise.

I can tell he's surprised at me. He looks aghast that I'm the same girl who has been so pleasant during our long walks and dinner table talks.

"Okay, Laurel. Discard those weighty hardcovers and keep the paperbacks."

I still persist in negotiating the right to estimate the weight of some bulkier books and sacrifice a like amount of softcovers. When Richard shrugs that he doesn't care, I sit on the floor like a hangman determining what lives with me and what goes. I can feel that I won my way, but lost something in his attitude toward me.

"Hey, look at this." I hold up a black Bible that was once given to me in a fourth-grade Sunday school. "Should I dump it?"

When, he says, "Oh," in a cold voice that's the fulcrum between opposite answers, I toss it on the pile that I'm keeping. It is a kind of history book, an unusual record of an ancient age.

I'm sorry to see Mother has included my high-school yearbooks. I can see an orange-and-black "1963" on top of a stack, almost like a record of reincarnation, of a past life in which I purposely back-combed my hair to give me four inches of body over each ear.

After filling four boxes of discards, I stagger under the weight of them to Triple's front porch. It seems late enough now to knock. Surprisingly the door has been left open about the width of a foot. I knock and call my friend's name through the crack. Triple's approaching footsteps stop as I hear a single-syllable swear word, then the sound of clicking boots resumes down the hall to the door.

"I got two new dogs," says Triple, in his greeting, while coming out on the porch to pick a fistful of pages from a stack of newspapers.

"I'm afraid they choose to urinate everywhere but on the printed page. They should belong to a journalist."

Triple's wearing a maroon satin dressing gown with thick-soled shoes.

"I finally got your rings done. Come and look."

Just stepping in the door, I can touch the puppies. They look like collies covered with a golden down. As I pat them, I can see a trail of newspapers and the puddle that produced the strong oath.

"Laurel, go up the stairs. The rings are somewhere on my workbench in the first room you'll see at the top."

I've never been to his upper floor. One could pencil messages in the dust at the ends of each tread. Below me the dogs try to follow but are too small and uncoordinated to climb a step.

The workbench is under a platform suspended from the ceiling by chains, and on top is Triple's mattress. There are marks where two of the walls have been scraped.

I look among the tools and supplies and find our rings. The bands are silver and border a rectangle of polished wood. Three silver dots are set in the mahogany. I admire them while slipping on the one with the smallest circumference.

On the stairs I can hear that Richard has come inside. His voice mingles with the sound of the cast-iron door being opened and bumped by logs for the wood stove.

Not waiting for my expression, Triple asks what I think. Handing Richard his, I let him exclaim with me.

"I want to also give you something else," says Triple. "You are going to need a dog for Alaska, and I want you to take one of these."

Richard is about to refuse, but I'm faster.

"I would love a puppy," I exclaim, reaching down to the dogs who are biting at each other at my feet. Delighted that my husband is not protesting, I separate one and lift him to my lap for a closer inspection. Now in my arms he needs a name. All immediate offerings are dull. Richard's suggestions are too foreign, like the title astronomers might bestow on a discovered star. It's Triple who wins. He cries out, slapping his knee, "You guys in that house should have a dog named Noah!"

59

As our host has our attention he continues with a completely new topic. He looks Richard in the eyes. "Why don't you wait here for spring and get a better financial grubstake? Choosing the three coldest months to drive to Alaska doesn't sound like the best plan."

It sounds funny to hear such practicality from a man who has filled his living room with round cross sections of trees nailed onto squat supporting trunks. The design looks like toadstools against walls that are an unfinished mural of high grass. Open paint cans and brushes are at the end, farthest from the fire.

"We'll only need a month by your house and in local parks to complete the interior. We don't have a lot of money, but once we start we can just work our way north." I'm surprised at Richard's voice. It sounds almost fierce with determination. I look at my husband, wondering at his tone.

"Yes, we have to continue on," I state in agreement.

I'm sobered by the glimpse of myself I've had this morning. I'm just as capable of plucking us down as a couple as I am of building us up. My independent nature can make marriage hard work.

WASHINGTON
January 5, 1967

The truck cab feels like a kind of double saddle as I sit next to Richard with Noah on my lap. As I look out into the roadside woods, whose banks are crusted with old snow, it seems almost impossible that we are finally under way, and one state farther north.

We had to be weaned of Portland as if it were the giant breast that nurtured us. A series of small overnight shakedown trips were only sips from the cup; we always returned to the familiar bosom. Now, there's nothing but the road north.

"What is that on the dashboard?" Richard's voice has such a sarcastic lift that I look at him. He's dabbing the ends of his new moustache with his tongue where the hairs protrude over his lip.

I reply that it is a rock, with deliberate enunciation of each of my one-syllable words.

"No," says Richard.

On one of our trial runs I had suggested collecting things on our dashboard. It would take awhile, but I could assemble a wedge of colored stones, feathers, and evergreen branches that still had pinecones attached. It was never a serious argument, yet it was still a matching of wills.

"Okay, Richard, I was just admiring the rock and left it there. I have the right to put things on my side."

We have the leisure of at least two thousand miles ahead for dialogues big and small.

"Sure," replies my husband. "One sudden stop, and it's on our laps."

I have to laugh. Our conversation has turned into a kind of checkers game, and my last marker was just jumped. As a good loser I crack open my window and throw out the stone. There is no snow now except for a ground cover of frost in the areas that remain mostly in shadow. I notice the highway signs are a white silhouette of George Washington's head.

"Look Richard, there's a lot of warmth and light on our dashboard. Custom-build a small planter box that we can secure on each side. Then, let's press in marijuana seeds among common garden flowers like pansies that never reach any height."

"There's a policeman following us."

I can see my husband glancing up from the road to look in his side mirror.

"He can't touch us, Richard. We are fifteen miles below the speed limit." Yet I still feel nervous. Maybe there's a new radar device that just hones in on the spoken word "drugs." I try to concentrate on the intricate network of tree limbs against the sky, but my meditation is punctured by the siren. In my side mirror I can see the red-and-blue revolving light as Richard releases his foot from the gas and looks for an adequate shoulder for our vehicle.

The cop who walks to Richard's window is void of expression

as he asks for the driver's license and registration. He's like a robot in a uniform with an authoritative voice and an inability to smile. The dog stands up, and nose to our company, wags his tail.

"He just wants to hassle us," says Richard grimly, as he watches the policeman take the identification back to his vehicle to run a check.

I feel angry that we should be victimized just because we are

different. My father, who drives a new Buick station wagon, would never be stopped. It isn't fair that there's pressure exerted on those who choose to live on the edges of the bell-shaped curve of normal.

The policeman is back with a yellow-and-white-layered ticket separated by a carbon. "It's against regulations not to have mud flaps on this size truck. You'll find the fines listed on the back."

"Oh, give us a break," I ask. "We'll just go and correct this today."

I'm trying to address some human particle in him. Maybe once he loved his grandmother, played with a dog, got a present for Christmas.

"Can't do that. Once a ticket is written up, it's in the books."

We just sit there in frustrated rage as the policeman goes back to his squad car and drives away on the road ahead of us. I can feel hate in me. It comes from being punched by something bigger than we are.

Richard looks for the fine first, then not finding it, passes the forms to me. There's a whole list of snares and costs like expired parking meters and stopping at the wrong-colored curb. Under "Heavy-duty Vehicles" is a twenty-five-dollar charge for not having mud flaps.

"You know," says Richard, "if this isn't paid, the fine doubles, and it would eventually go to warrant for my arrest. We have no choice but to buy a money order and envelope in the next town."

I immediately translate this new cost into the medium of grocery prices. "This county is stealing two weeks of our food!"

"And almost half the money we have on hand," says Richard.

"We've got to get to Alaska!"

The thought of the comparative freedom of the wilderness is our one consolation as Richard turns the key in the ignition. I think of the truck now as the *Mayflower*; we must sail to some shore where we can be free.

There are some construction sites in the trees, which multiply until the forest dissolves into a housing tract as we come into Olympia. The capitol building is a shiny dome in the small city vista.

Richard indicates a riverbank where we can park with a view. His idea is to later today fold and attach black roofing paper flaps over the rear tires. My first duty in making camp will be to insert our stovepipe so it rises above the roof. I'll start a fire and from our sack of fifty pounds of potatoes put four in for our meal.

Richard's just pulled out the small access ladder to the front door when a green-and-white city police car pulls alongside us. We freeze, neither speaking or moving. Only the dog is animated. I call him back, knowing he might lift a leg or lower his haunches to relieve himself. I am fearing another ticket; they may fine a dog that fouls the footway.

"Some rig you got there. But there's no camping allowed in city limits, folks."

Richard indicates that he's glad to move, then asks if there's any place where it would be lawful to stay.

"May as well lead you myself," says the young patrolman. "We have a state park that's mostly vacant in winter."

Collapsing the stovepipe, Richard lays it back on the floor of the cabin, while I put the ladder next to it. I whisper that Richard should whistle the "Star-Spangled Banner" as a subtle endorsement of us as Americans of integrity. Instead my husband uses a false, cheerful voice in thanking the law for help.

Back in the cab, I notice that, now with a police escort, cars change lanes to give us room. I feel like being absurd. My impulse is to prop our dog on the window and move one of his paws in the motion of a mock greeting. Yet I fear this could be seen in the cop's rearview mirror, so I try to sit as if I'm part of a UN delegation being ushered through New York City.

One pocket-sized book I took from Import Warehouse is a collection of Zen aphorisms. I keep it in the glove box for the times I want a little snack of language. Feeling people staring at us from windows on all three sides, I take it out as occupation for my bowed head. Opening at random I read, "Only those who appreciate the least palatable of the vegetable roots know the meaning of life."

At a stoplight, I wonder again if there really is a meaning, or are all the spokesmen of enlightenment like the emperor in his new clothes. The adherents chant how beautiful they are clothed in their philosophies, but they just might be naked and know nothing.

Still self-conscious, I keep my head down now patting the dog until we are off the main street and back again in the country.

January 15

Unfurled, the map of Washington has fluttered between Richard and me like some bird with a broad wingspan. Sometimes, with one edge unfolded, it's more like a small sparrow flying from my hand to his. I can see by the spot denoting Tacoma that it will be a larger town than Olympia.

"Do you think we stayed too long?"

"Probably," replies Richard.

We camped in the state park for a week. It was like a long, pleasant dream being alone in the woods. The variations in temperature released snow in clumps from the overhanging branches, making plopping sounds on our roof. I experimented with bread recipes, naming most of the loaves after national

parks like Old Smokey, and Crater Lake. My husband built things. He constructed a hinged ladder that could be unfolded to climb up into the loft.

"Richard, didn't it feel like we were playing house among those firs, rather than really keeping one? We just needed Triple to come and pretend he was the Avon lady."

Richard replies in a half-measure laugh.

"What is very real is the gas gauge. We're close to empty. Look, Laurel, after paying the state its fine and buying fuel and groceries, we have depleted almost all our cash."

Immediately I think about us getting in line behind the seven dwarfs who are off to the mine singing, "Hi ho, hi ho, it's off to work we go . . ."

We take the freeway exit to city center. Tacoma is built on the shore of Puget Sound. I can see a pine-covered island in the inlet and guess that the Cascade Mountains would be visible if the day weren't overcast.

Driving down a street that includes boarded-up storefronts, small bars, and an adult movie house, Richard sees a pawn shop.

"Your parents sent us a camera for Christmas. Let's just exchange it for cash to hold us until we're working. It's worth an immediate five dollars."

"No," I cry, feeling alarmed.

"Look, Laurel, how could we ever pay for film and developing pictures, anyway?"

It's not a matter of logic. I don't want to let go of the camera. It's to record the land we'll claim and the house we'll build. My throat is constricting, holding back my tears as Richard looks for a curbside parking place.

"It's pretty slick how we can use these truck zones!"

I won't even talk. I note that he isn't promoting the idea that we can buy it back later. My typewriter is still in Portland. It was far more important to me than the drum he sacrificed for money.

Some Indians are leaning against a wall staring at us. One is holding a brown bag that I guess covers a bottle they are passing among them. I hate poverty. Richard climbs out to seek the camera in the back, while I remember him suggesting we leave it intact in the box as soon as we'd opened it. I wonder if the Noel wrapping paper was still in my hands when he started calculating how to protect it for resale.

The anger in me has prongs. I've already attached one hook into how I'm regarding my husband. Yet as I watch him walking with his shoulders rolled forward while he carries the Kodak box, I feel sorry for him. His foster-home childhood never let him feel anything really belonged to him.

Now, it's self-pity that has me. I'll never again be able to turn over the price tag on a shirt and buy it. Only the rich have admission money for movies, or can order food from restaurant menus. Not wanting those solemn-eyed men to witness my tears, I get out of the truck to walk in the opposite direction from my husband.

The sidewalk is dirty. Amidst all the boarded exteriors, one shop has been renovated. I can see geraniums in pots along the window. *The Salvation Army Rescue Mission* is painted on the glass in precise gold lettering. Opening the door, I see a man in a shiny-buttoned uniform sitting at a desk. In front of him is a lopsided circle of old, comfortable furniture. Religious art decorates the walls. Every picture is of the crucified Christ in agony.

"What do you do?" I blurt in response to his welcoming nod. I immediately fear he'll answer by firing a continuous round of Bible versus at me. I'll be driven out to the street by gospel bullets and stand and drink with the Indians.

"We're here to help anyone with a real need."

Since I'm still staggering in the mire of self-pity, I don't have my usual assured footing. I ask if he will hire my husband and me for five dollars' worth of labor. I choose Richard's estimate of the camera's value in pawn.

"Sure," he replies. "One of you can wash my car, and I have a stack of envelopes that need stamps."

After assuring him I'll be back, I race for Richard, hoping I can spare the Kodak. He's already in the truck resting one elbow on the steering wheel. At my appearance he raises four fingers to communicate that the deed is done, and the yield.

I, in turn, tell of our chance for a thirty-minute employment. Richard follows me, relieved that my emotions have not escalated to a downpour from the storm warnings he first saw. I lead us inside and at ramrod attention execute a mock salute.

The Salvation Army man has organized a bucket and sponge for my husband and a pile of mail for me. Again, I'm relieved that we can just start to work without having to listen to some tape-recorded speech by Billy Graham.

After collecting five one-dollar bills we get in the truck to immediately buy gas. Our financial life is like first-grade math. The Chevron pump, registering five, must be subtracted from the ten in Richard's wallet. We have a five-dollar sum to put toward everything we want and need in the universe.

Looking for a parking place, we've learned that our vehicle has to be out of city limits. We choose a road that traces the water's edge. It passes a pier where I can see crates on shore stamped for Cam Ranh Bay, Vietnam. After passing a manufacturing company we find an empty expanse of cement. It is completely vacant; Richard surmises that it was originally intended for factory expansion but never got funding.

The truck is pulled as close to the water as possible so we can see the waves from our four windows. The water looks like shades of gray steel, appropriate for industrial zoning.

In the fading afternoon light, we both look for driftwood to start a fire. The dog runs around us making sounds like a seagull. We are almost silhouette figures that are moving in step, or more often, with one lagging behind to pick up a board from the short rise of pebbled beach. The wood feels like the incense sticks from the sea, pungent with brine.

There's no speech between us. In the quiet of our simple labor, I compare my marriage to a giant sifter; I've been pressed hard against its grate. So much that I considered necessity was really luxury, and it's gone. Today my camera, which I wanted to photograph our homestead with, has fallen through the grid, like my typewriter before it. Yet the pen and cheap notebook diary will always remain. I have no shower with a needle point massage spray head, but I still get clean with a cloth and buckets of water warmed on the stove.

I know myself better too, since undergoing the daily scrub of marriage. Illusions are popping like iridescent soap bubbles. I'm not as noble as I thought I would be. I can move more quickly to resentment than to kindness. When the soapy film of my personality dissolves, underneath is dirty water.

First thing in the truck I mix flour, yeast, salt, and water. Richard works the lantern, so I stir in the dark but knead in the light. While he moves his attention to the fire, I stretch the dough into a long flat loaf and mark its length with diagonal slashes. Our dishes are bright-colored tin. We are so quick to form habits: I always take a blue plate; he has the red.

After rinsing our utensils from the kettle, I want to read in bed. I leave Richard the lantern so he can have the best light for continuing to carve a coat hook, and I take the flashlight. Since the Zen proverbs are still in the cab, I pull out my old Bible. I feel like slow language.

Usually I undress by the fire, rotating my nude body like a planet in its orbit warmed by the sun. But my nightgown has been left under my pillow in a little wad of flowered flannel. I climb the ladder with one hand, and then crawl the few feet to our mattress. There's no room to rise much above my knees because of the sloping roof. I toss my corduroy pants and turtleneck over to the corner. At my feet is the water tank that we fill at intervals in gas stations. The sheets, a wedding gift, are a pattern of monotonous large orange dots. I've taken a pen and filled in some of the spots with whimsical faces on my side of the bed. My elbow is now resting on my drawing of a winking eye as I open the Bible.

The page has all the words printed in red. It's peculiar because I can see that the previous chapters are the standard black lettering. I can imagine laborers in a 1954 print shop running out of black ink and momentarily substituting crimson.

I want to pick out any paragraph, and let some old lines hum in me and then fall asleep. I remember the Bible, from the one time I tried to read it, as containing long lists of names. They were words that acted as bubble gum; my jaw was exercised by all the foreign syllables until I quit.

Not seeing any genealogy, I look at what appears to be instructions. I read, *"The measure of a man is not what he owns."*

Raising my head to the raw cedar in front of me, I'm surprised by the truth of it. It sounds almost revolutionary, like something that can be spray-painted in red as graffiti to confront suburbanites. I was expecting some list that commends roast beef for dinner but forbids a pork chop. I let my finger trace along the words of a new paragraph:

"But you, take no thought of what you eat, drink, or wear, like all the people of the nations."

I lay down the book, chuckling about what I've seen of modern Christianity. If all the churches are a boat, they have drifted far from the dock of these words.

Richard emerges onto the platform of the loft. I'd been too engrossed to hear him on the ladder. He carries with him the smell of smoke from the wood stove and a slight essence of kerosene. The one flashlight in my hand moves shadows across his cheek.

"Now, listen to this." I reread for him the two sentences that confront our society.

"Keep on going," says Richard, wadding his pillow up under his chin.

"But above all else, you seek first the kingdom of God, and His righteousness, and all the rest will be added unto you."

Neither of us speak. The words feel personal now, no longer for the groups outside, but for us alone together. It seems like more than a phrase on a page, a voice addressing us.

I decide that I have to quit reading what the italics at the top of the page state is the Sermon on the Mount, and I lay the book face down. I don't want cracks in my perception of reality. Everything is relative, and nothing is absolute. I want to laugh that I was touched, if only for a moment, by a Bible. I refuse to end up

like some old woman I once saw leaving scripture pamphlets in public bathroom stalls.

"Oh, come on," says Richard, "read some more." His voice is impatient. He's even gesturing while he speaks by flicking his hand.

Lifting the book back up, I continue to quote paragraphs in a voice a little louder than a whisper. Each passage convinces me further of the logic and purity of Christianity. It seems now to be such a well-made gown that I feel too unclean to ever put it on. It all makes me feel there is a God, and that I'm naked before him.

"This is ridiculous, Richard. There's no way anyone can wear the robe of being a Christian. It calls for perfection, and all of us are flawed!"

Richard put his hand on my arm. Holding the light directly at the page, I can hardly see him at all.

"But that has to be the point of the cross, Laurel."

I think of the two simple lines that intersect as a decoration on walls, on the tops of buildings, and suspended as bits of jewelry. I grasp that there is a flashing reality behind the symbol. It's in the words of ancient hymns. The refrain has always been a holy God and sinful human beings bridged by the atonement of his Son.

"You know, we have stolen almost everything."

Richard is not speaking to me. It's as though both of us are facing a mirror that reflects only our excessive greed, lust, and pride. I can't stand the sight of myself. I have spent my life rationalizing and forgetting.

I can feel Richard taking my hand, although it is wet from rubbing my eyes.

"Laurel, I think we must do something like ask to be forgiven."

Too overwhelmed to answer, I let him go first, and then take my turn to speak. We use simple words, not the colored language of stained-glass windows or the phrases of King James. Instead, we affirm belief; we yield our wills.

In the process of our expression, I feel the garment of Christ being pulled over our shoulders. I can feel that my mind and heart have received a royal robe. I am new, and what we are together can be a new configuration of a couple too.

I finally sleep, wrapped in the beauty of the words "Saviour" and "Father."

January 16

My blanket seems woven from gold and silver strands. My pillow is filled with flower petals. We may have died and may be resting in some heavenly bower with angels in attendance—who are beginning to talk loudly among themselves. Can wings get caught in the slamming of car doors? I hear the noise of motors and the voices of men calling to each other. I open my eyes, and in the morning light it's even louder. After waking Richard, I slip down from the loft. Out both windows I can see we are surrounded by vehicles. Richard slides down beside me and peers out.

"This has to be a company parking lot!"

I volunteer that it must be Monday. There's a throng of men dressed in the working clothes of assembly-line employees and in addition carrying dome-topped lunch buckets. Richard and I both remark that it doesn't look like we can move our rig because of the press of automobiles. The spaces between cars and the formation of rows is too irregular for navigating our International truck to the highway. I can see more vehicles still pouring in to park, filling up the far side.

"It looks like we're here to stay until 5:00 P.M.," chuckles Richard.

The day is clear. The band of clouds has dissipated, revealing blue skies. An uncharacteristic happiness still pervades. Usually I would feel some frustration at being trapped, but instead I'm reacting to the day shift as part of the natural order of things. Richard moves from the window to start the fire. It's the first act of morning—equivalent to blowing a bugle and raising the flag.

I quickly dress to take the dog to the beach. Standing outside, I can see across the water snow-capped mountains that overcast skies earlier concealed. I marvel at the transformation of my mind. Everything, from sand grain to galaxies made invisible by the sun, has meaning. God created the heavens and the earth.

Finally, I turn back upon hearing Richard's voice. It's unusual for him to be calling my name. Clapping my hands to alert Noah, I start toward our cabin, which is elevated above the mass of colored metal roofs.

Richard is obviously relieved to see me. He's leaning out the doorway and motioning me to haste. I know I've been gone well over an hour, but my long walks have never before disturbed him.

"We have company," he announces to me in a voice trying to sound casual, but I feel panic crouching behind the fence of his words.

"Laurel, these people are from Tacoma's newspaper."

Looking up, I can see a couple standing behind Richard. The man has an expensive-looking camera around his neck, and the woman is holding a briefcase. I feel like making jokes about the *Daily Planet*, Lois Lane, and Jimmy, but I'm intimidated by their appearance. Once in the house, I perceive that Richard must have kept himself occupied while waiting for me by putting wood on the fire. The room is unbearably hot and with four standing adults it is as tiny as a closet.

"We got a call from the Northern Line Engineering Company that your camper had been seen in their auxiliary parking lot. We just think there might be a human interest story here."

I look at the journalist, who, like me, is in her early twenties. I surmise that she has both a checking and a savings account. She's wearing a rich suede coat with purple leather trim. The jewelry on her fingers, wrist, neck, and ears salutes the arts. She likes the medium of wide gold. By contrast I feel unkempt, with my hair hanging down like two spaniel's ears and clad in a boxy plaid raincoat that I wore in high school.

Maybe we were in the same stream while growing up, but all rivers fork with decisions. And this woman, now opening a stenographer's pad, went one direction and I another. I can feel the gulf as her lead question asks for our credentials. She wants to know where Richard went to college.

"UCLA," I blurt. Having chosen a false shiny engine, it's easy to couple behind it a whole train of partial answers.

"So your major area of study is theology," the reporter repeats. Even my body feels off track. The gossamer peace that had let me float from minute to minute is gone. I am full of weight and in some pricking nettles.

"We're both writers," injects Richard, "although I'm just starting."

"So you publish?" she asks.

"Just me," I add. "A children's book."

With our past now reduced to lines of fiction, the reporter asks about our plans. Richard says he would like to take the ferry to Seward. "I don't think I'm much for that Arctic Circle stuff."

Never having heard him discuss any alternative other than the gravel highway through the Canadian Yukon, I stare in surprise.

The photographer requests us to step outside for some shots. Following the woman out the door, I can see the cloud cover is beginning to wrap the sky again in white gauze. The photographer gives instructions. We are moved around the stage visible only to him through his Nikon lens. Feeling guilty about my fabrications, I mock myself with the fear that he might ask us to hold up our college diplomas.

"Is there anything else you want to add?"

I know it's the last chance to state what sounds foolish and trite: we have found it to be true that Christ is the only way to God. Yet I stand instead in mute misery. My vanity has just won the race against any declaration of faith. As they walk away to a late model car, I feel wretched from the paradox of my performance. The things that should have been shared, I kept silent, and all the statements that should never have been made were fluently expressed.

After exhaling that he is glad that is over, Richard wants to go down to the beach. I watch my husband walk out of sight between bumpers and car hoods.

Climbing back up into the cabin, I fill pans with water to use the radiating heat of the stove. From my last night's experience I feel like a living cupboard that now holds the real milk and meat that people are starving for. I kept it locked and only threw out one dry bone in the word "theology." Undressing for a sponge bath, I can see the practice of Christianity is going to take much more than sincere intention.

In the weak light of late Monday, the cars begin to move. From the window it reminds me of a frozen lake thawing with the turn of motor and ignition. We hasten to join the flow to the highway and turn with one of the streams toward town.

"Let's experiment with coal! I think we can bank it through the night, and unlike wood, it'll still have heat in the morning."

Richard spotted a fuel yard on our first drive through Tacoma. He's convinced it will be an investment of just small change for our experiment. Looking over at my husband, I know he carries the burden of navigating a cabin into below-zero temperatures, without a wood pile. Often he has expressed concern that the whole water tank could freeze in a night.

Even with the window rolled up, I can smell the acrid odor of coal. There are dark piles throughout the yard from large trucks dumping coal in towering heaps. I choose to sit and wait, with Noah on my lap like a living muff. The street has one gas station and some flashing neon from a lone café. The restaurant looks to me like the kind of place that has a large inventory of frozen hamburger patties and pancake mix.

It all adds to my sense of loneliness. I can feel it in the strains of a freight train whistle and in the bark of a dog sounding chained for the night far from the house.

"Hey," Richard opens my door. He lifts the dog from my arms and puts him on the ground. "We can earn some quick cash tonight! They need some small gunnysacks filled with coal, and we'll be paid by the number we can stuff. The manager says we can just camp behind the gates here."

I reserve my enthusiasm until I can see the size of the burlap bag. A breeze is cold upon my face, and the mercury lights in the yard provide a surreal illumination. Everything smells like a London street after the Industrial Revolution. Richard shows me a pile of bags that I estimate, from potato packages in markets, to hold close to fifty pounds.

Fetching my gloves from the truck, I look at the new gray cloth palms and sweater-knit fingers. My parents sent them last month at Christmas; I would rather soil my hands.

The coal is cold. Squatting on my haunches I feel I deserve both the dirt and the labor. I lied to the newspaper, and it's an ancient tale that children who are bad get these lumps of carbon in their stocking.

Abstractly, I wonder what would have been our fate if I had told the truth and talked like a Baptist bookstore. I decide that the day could have held an opposite destiny. We could have been enlisted for an emergency round-trip flight to the south to pluck a bumper crop of cherries in a scented orchard.

January 17

We have money. A portion is declared for food once Richard gets the check from the coal yard. Twenty dollars gives me the enthusiasm to even take a cart. With just change to spend, all the goods can be suspended in one arm. It's easy then to rove the aisles always seeing what I can't have. Now, I am in a celebration, real hamburger, not my protein source pinto beans. I lay three packages of meat across the cart's toddler bench and abandon myself to the pleasure of studying the flavors of the large store-brand sodas on sale at five for a dollar.

Richard's waiting in the truck cab. He sacked coal long after I washed my arms and went to bed. He has no energy, just the wish to find a truly isolated parking spot along Puget Sound. Back in our vehicle, I put the grocery sacks at my feet. I want to feel crowded by food; I like Campbell soup cans leaning against my calf. I can easily imagine myself at forty hoarding case goods and refusing to waste any leftover crumb.

We find a shoreline without factory or fisherman. Behind us, in the distance, is a cliff with a few apartment units that provide living-room views of the sea. Adjusting our rig we pull onto the sand where we are more than a high-tide's reach from the water. My husband goes right from turning off the motor to lighting tinder in our stove.

I'm hoping Richard isn't too tired to talk. I want us as a couple to feel like more than joint operators of food and heat. I wait until we can't see our breath and our coats can go back to the pegs on the door. I wait until the kettle heats and he has tea.

"Something really happened to us, Richard. I'm changed from that night."

As he nods back in agreement, eyes to mine, I realize we have no words of explanation, nor have we ever heard of anyone else who's experienced what we did.

"It's like my conscience is alive," I state, looking down at the coal dust still embedded in the crevices of my hand.

Lying had never bothered me before, or guilt of such duration that I could still feel it ticking. Fabrications before had always been the art of creating lines for convenience or flourish.

"You did make us sound like we're driving north wearing mortarboards and gowns."

The old Richard would have laughed, but he too is sober from his new birth of ethics.

"So, what can we do about it now?" he asks with a shrug.

"Look around us, Richard. Divide in your mind what we took and what was really given to us." My words create a kind of balance, and I can mentally separate gifts from theft, honor from dishonor.

"Even my hammer," says Richard, rising from the chair. "I picked it up at a construction site," he says while turning it in his hand. Opening the door, he slings the tool out onto the sand.

"What are you doing? We've been forgiven!"

"Look, Laurel, we can't drive back to Portland, Los Angeles, or your Berkeley library and return this stuff. What we can do is put everything out there visible on the rocks. Think of it as a gesture of giving it all back by giving it away."

He is animated and is acting as if he is lighter than air.

"I think the whole point, Laurel, is to show what we believe by what we try to do."

It seems to me far out and radical, yet I'm flooded with a sense of respect for my husband stronger than I have ever felt before. I begin gathering up the boxes of candles first, and my emotions border on hilarity.

I carry our matching raw wool sweaters out to the rocks and fold the arms across the chest. I'm careful with the books too, so they can't slide down and fray any pages. It's not a fast job. We both have a long past of gathering petty merchandise. Richard carries out the bags of flour that he took from the ice cream cone factory. The sun is heavy on the horizon, and the water seems to have little flecks of electricity through its currents. The birds circle along the shoreline, and I assume we are a disappointment; there are no fish heads or tails in our business.

"Laurel, we still have the chairs and the mattress." I clearly acknowledge we stole them from Mrs. Spicklemire's basement, yet I'm not enthusiastic at losing their comfort. My body has a distinct voice for where it wants to sit and sleep.

Following Richard inside, I climb up to the loft to quickly strip the bed of its sheet and blankets. While maneuvering the bulk of the mattress, and attempting to fold it like a giant piece of sandwich bread through the opening, Richard's eyes look up from his work. His gaze sweeps past me.

"You know, that water tank was hoisted too. I had some guys from the factory help me get it down from a lot where they were tearing down houses."

My arms lose, for a second, their strength in my labor.

"Does the tank have to go too?" My voice has little volume. All that I can think of is hauling water and storing it in covered buckets. I have taken my gravity-fed faucets for granted.

"Look Laurel, we want this to be the clean start of a completely new life. I even bet we'll recover these things that we are now giving up, but in a right way."

I can hear my husband turning on the sink taps to drain the weight from the tank. My immediate instruction is for him to see what containers there are and preserve some of that water. There are already cups needing washing, and the dinner plates and pots are ahead.

The late afternoon winter sun is feeble as we finish our peculiar cleansing. At times it has looked as though there would be more outside than left within. I wonder who will be walking along the dunes and rocks to find these things, a strange array of dry and perfect treasures washed up by the sea. Surveying some of the small trinkets swiped from Import Warehouse, I think of a children's story plot to explain it. The Northwest mermaids have labored to give these gifts to the people that inhabit the shores of their waters. Now needing a sign, I print FREE in large letters on a blank page that ripped from my diary.

There's still hot tea on the stove. While stripping the house Richard must have kept adding wood scraps to the fire. This time we have nothing to sit on around our windowsill table.

"I doubt if it's even five yet, but let's go up to bed anyway, Laurel."

I look at my husband leaning against the bookcase and see that he's exhausted beyond any idea of waiting for dinner. Turning to take our tinware to the sink, I'm startled by seeing a section of a rainbow. Its prism is etched on the face of our cast-iron stove. Richard exclaims at the distinct colors at the same time I'm pointing to it. I'm sure a scientist could list the angle of the afternoon light rays refracting through the curvature of our kerosene lamp globe, but to us, it is a sign and wonder. Hesitant to leave, we finally climb to bed in silence. We each are locked into our own devotions.

It is warm in the loft and dusty where the tank has been. We cannot afford to use many blankets for padding underneath us, as the upstairs heat is as transitory as embers. One old cover, given to us from my parent's linen closet, goes under the sheet. The orange dot pattern wrinkles at both ends with no mattress to fill the elasticized fitted corners. Bare earth can yield for bony hips, but boards are resolute. I speculate on the long hard nights ahead unless we can find some thrift shop with a fumigated mattress. Richard's already asleep. I turn from my side where we fit together, our knees indenting at the same angle, to lie now on my back.

I can hear a car pull up outside our truck and stop. As its motor idles, there is knocking at our door, not a timid pecking, but a firm, loud rap. What if it's the police, I think, and we're getting a citation for littering?

Climbing over Richard, who is also stirring, I lower myself to the door.

"Hi, I'm Bill Roedecker, and this is my wife, Anne. We live in those apartments." He gestures to the buildings on the bluff. "Well, we saw your picture in tonight's paper and thought why not come down and ask you for dinner."

Richard has joined me. Reaching out his hand, he gives our names. It's funny sometimes being a woman. Men take the handlebars, and we're on the side seat. Afraid that Richard will politely refuse, I insert a yes to their offer of hospitality.

Following them to their car, I can see that Bill and Anne are much older than we are; silver shades their locks. Richard wants to know about the Tacoma newspaper story. All the colors of our goods on the rocks are shrouded by night into dark shadows.

"You're on the front page, kids, and since we don't believe in coincidences, we wanted to have you come on up."

Anne speaks of the simple meal. "It's just homemade chili and hot bread," she says, while turning in the seat to speak to me.

The Roedecker's warmth makes their apartment homey. They act like relatives and not strangers, offering us the use of their shower. We both grab for that gold ring of unlimited warm water coursing out of a shower head. I let my husband go first and walk into the living room. It is full of handmade things; there are afghans in the bright colors of Woolworth's yarn. The pillows, too, are home-quilted with shiny polyester scraps. There is a moonlit seascape above the couch. It belongs in a place like Kansas, not where one can turn a head and compare oils to life.

Anne brings me the night's paper. It is shocking to see our black-and-white image square on the front page below the caption "City Couple Lugging Home to Quiet Alaska." I had assumed we would be in an auxiliary section. There just hadn't been any hijacked airlines or assassination attempts to move us to a proper back page.

When Richard emerges, his head glossy with water and furrowed by a comb, I hand it to him and seek the bathroom for myself.

I find it so full of steam it could grow jungle plants. The mirror is a shiny sphere of moisture. I strip and turn my underpants inside out to partially compensate for my lack of clean clothes.

Once in the water I'm full of harmony with a repetitive lyric of giving thanks. There's nothing mechanical in singing the same thing over and over. Joy swells in devotion.

Anne lights candles and direct us to chairs. The tapers show every evidence of nightly use; they are almost stubs in their glass containers. Bill reaches for Richard's and his wife's hands, while Anne takes mine. My husband and I fumble with each other's knuckles, a little unsure of this procedure. As our host utters a sincere grace, I glimpse that we are not the only ones whose attention has been tapped by God. There must be quite a family at large.

Bill tells us that he and his wife have moved from the country to the city to start a new business. They are beginning to manufacture rocking horses. Richard replies that most likely we are back to the business of driving north in the morning.

January 18

New lanes keep adding to the width of the freeway before Seattle. By the time the city skyline is visible there are six of them for traffic in either direction. Every vehicle goes faster than our International, pushing its maximum of 45.

Richard and I are largely silent. Remarking on the urban density, our exchanges are limited to half and quarter phrases. On the freeway high above Seattle, we are debating which off ramp our truck should take down into the pool of the city.

"Not here," says Richard. "Looks like it's all parking meters!"

Our rig pushes past the high buildings of Seattle. Each exit that we reject I turn into a story of a missed destiny. Glimpsing a doughnut house, I pretend that we obtained employment and I gained a hundred pounds.

The city turns to suburbs, and we never veer from the freeway. Both of us are tired from sleeping on the loft's wooden floor. For me it is like floating on the top of sleep with never any real immersion. I spend the night imagining all the possible fiber contents of mattresses.

"Everett looks good, Laurel."

It's the first town north of Seattle. Looking for a parking place I wonder how many tree limbs birds survey to find a crook for their nests. What do rabbits look for before their forepaws scratch out warren tunnels? We want views of water. Richard pulls our home over three parking stripes at the Everett yacht club. The adjacent wharf is lined with fishing boats bobbing in the current.

I jump from the truck proposing that we first seek a thrift shop. Most of our silverware had left Import Warehouse in my pockets and so was abandoned in the purge. I know that I can buy forks out of bins for pennies.

"What artful variety, Richard, to have each utensil be a completely different pattern."

My husband doesn't answer or open our house door. Instead, he takes my arm and strolls with me along the dock. My eye contrasts the working boats with the sleek pleasure craft.

"If it's a Salvation Army thrift store maybe we could exchange work again for, say, a mattress. I would love to sort and categorize donation boxes."

Making no reply, Richard pauses to watch a man sitting beside an open tackle box with his fishing rod.

"Think about restaurants, Richard. Within hours there's always a pocketful of coins on a table." Now putting up two fingers I list the second advantage, courtesy meals for employees.

"And three, there is at least a minimum-wage paycheck."

"I don't know," he replies.

"Oh, come on Richard," I retort, feeling irritated by his inactivity when we have so many pressing needs. "It could give me an opportunity to bring my faith into my work. I've never seen anyone offer a prayer of thanks before they eat, the way the Roedeckers did. That could be my special contribution. I'll serve the plates and say a silent grace for each customer. And waitresses have liberty in arranging food on plates. I'll always design a cross out of french fries. You might think of it as a visual provoking."

"Oh, crazy!" laughs my husband. "What I want to do is to look for a church first before we make any other plans."

We pivot with his words. Seagulls rise and fall along the horizon. The birds are moving in lines like the rapid scribble marks that tiny children use to cover pages.

It's easy to find a church, but not as easy to find one with unlocked doors. After two attempts Richard waits in the truck while I run up the wide sidewalks to tug on all manner of unrelenting handles. I know there are different denominations, each with their own subtleties and emphasis, but I know nothing more. I have no experience to help me define the difference between Baptist or Lutheran. I've even stopped reading the signs by the time my pressure finally pulls open a door and reveals a vestibule. Motioning first to my husband, I walk inside feeling a hush of respect. It is easier to whisper in here than talk. I want it to be a little like the movies with a couple of widows in corner pews. But there's no one else in the sanctuary. There's a padded kneeling bench up by the altar. Following Richard, I go to the front and rest on my knees with my hands on the rail. I choose distance between us.

My prayer is a little like the lines on a postcard. I have a few sentences to express thank you, and a few more requesting for us to be led.

My attention is commanded by two stained-glass windows. I don't want to shut my eyes. Radiating with colored glass, the thin lead lines spiral out from the first Greek letter and the last. The alpha on one side and the omega on the other seem to compose the eyes of God, who sees from beginning to end.

Richard breaks the silence, "You know what we're going to do?" He leaves no pause for me to guess.

"We're going to sell everything we own and just trust in the Lord."

Stunned by his proposal, I say nothing. It's either silence on my part or shouting at him. No one can remain kneeling either making or hearing a proposal like this. Everything had been peace and order minutes before. I had been feeling that we were about to find a thrift store with small-change prices. Now I am outraged—and afraid. Richard has announced this in his cast-iron voice, the tone that leaves no room for debate. Strong emotion strips me of my powers of observation. I can no longer see carpet or wood grain as I stride to the door. Partly from my feelings, partly from the light outside, I throw my hands across my eyes.

"No, we can't give up everything! This is our truck, Richard, and our dream." I am crying. Already I know that every argument that I can produce is hopeless. My next question, "Why," wavers from my mouth.

"A lot of the roofing materials were stolen, for one thing, and we also need to tell our friends and family what we experienced. It could happen to them too."

"I can write letters, Richard, and we can work here to send back the money for those construction materials." I glare at my husband.

Then I turn and look at the truck. It was always going to be a part of my life. It would have its own half acre on our homestead site. I would walk with my grandchildren through Alaska woods and point to it, saying, "We came here in that all those years ago." Sentimentality releases another reservoir of tears.

Richard is kind, but firm. I hate for him to state, "This is what we are supposed to do." It doesn't seem fair for him to be bringing in the Invisible for credentials. I think he is calling his own impulsive notion "the leading of God."

Aware of cars driving by, I seek asylum in the truck cab. Leaning my head against the side window I keep my back to Richard, who climbs behind the steering wheel. He says nothing; nor does he start the motor.

My emotions feel as if torn by the little sharp teeth of a saw blade. My thoughts are all wood where I need a rock that nothing can cut. My concept of God has changed; I now perceive him as being personal and accessible. Now, I have to see him as so involved with my life and caring about it so much that if Richard is wrong, as I suspect, then the Lord will make it work out right. Anything short of this will continue to keep me in pain.

"What next?" I ask, but still refuse to turn and look at Richard.

"We are going to find an auto dealer or trailer mart and sell this rig." Richard starts the ignition.

"Are we ever going to Alaska?" I know my husband's answer is either going to be a crown of thorns for my head, or the balm of hope there will be flowers on the tree from which the thorns come.

"Sure, Honey. Let's hitchhike up there in the summer. By then we'll have more money." I can look at him now, wanting my eyes to seal it as a promise.

Richard chooses a used-vehicle dealer who has an immense lot to the side of a glass showroom. Seeing salesmen with suits inside, I watch my husband's progress through their door, his conversation with them, and then the employees' motioning to a manager.

Dropping my gaze, I pick off a dog hair from the corduroy grooves of my pants. I have the same feeling I've known in doctor's offices when a shot is being prepared and in moments the needle is going to enter my arm. As Richard opens the cab I wonder how much this is going to hurt.

"I have a hundred and fifty dollars in cash. We don't even have to bother with a check. Let's pack what we want to carry with us."

I didn't imagine that the feeling would be amputation, not inoculation. Following Richard, I try not to think that this is the last time I'll touch this door handle, feel the distance to the curb, hear the sound of our house door opening.

Taking a pillowcase from the loft, I must choose the few things that I can carry with me. Everything practical can be replaced, there are billions of bread pans. What I can't easily duplicate are my peculiar pieces of art. Opening my antique tin for "plug slice smoking tobacco" I put in it my rock fossil imprinted with a fern and my blue wedding brooch. I prop my *Moby Dick* drawings along the side of the bag to keep them from being crushed. My Bible comes and notebooks and other special goods. It all weighs too much to go on the end of a stick like my hobo costume of Halloweens past. Instead, I hug it all in my arms as I climb outside.

We have to walk. I can't bear to stand and hitchhike so close to our cabin's front door. Yet, thirty feet away from my last and lost home, a pale blue Thunderbird pulls to the roadside.

"Thought you kids could use a ride."

Since neither of us solicited transportation, it feels like Providence. After putting the dog at his feet, Richard puts his arms around my shoulders. With our acceleration to the highway, I look back. That last view provokes the kind of tears that have no sound but shake shoulders and chest. Richard whispers, for consolation, that he can build it all again.

"I'm heading for Portland, kids."

Richard acknowledges that this is also our destination, and the driver and passengers settle into a long-distance silence.

A post on the Columbia River bridge welcomes us back to Oregon. Continual signs enforce a lowering of legal vehicle speed until we enter the city at a few miles per hour. The driver chooses the center passageway of Portland's park blocks.

There are no more leaves. By January they have decomposed

into ground mulch. The benches that line the walkway are abandoned due to winter temperatures.

"Hey, Laurel, isn't that Karen walking over there with someone?"

I look where Richard is gesturing and see my old friend, who worked one of the cash registers at Import Warehouse.

"Oh, please let us off here," I request, while lifting up my pillowcase bundle. Leaving the thank you threads for Richard to tie, I bound up the curve waving. Karen sees us. She's walking with her boyfriend, whom I remember as having intense blue eyes and being her exact height.

"You've met Jack before," she says in greeting. I remember him coming to get Karen once at Import Warehouse's employee room. We had just finished between us a tin of smoked oysters that I had pocketed from a downstairs gourmet shelf. Her breath must have been like the bottom of a polluted sea, but he kissed her anyway with long tenderness.

"Where's your truck? We're living together now. Can you come over? I'm still checking Taiwan imports at the old cash register." Pushing some strands of blonde hair back under her wool cap, Karen utters every sentence with an enthusiasm that brackets them into a single paragraph.

We follow the couple to a small apartment house that looks as though it was built after World War II. There's no real lobby, but just enough space to shake the weather from one's coat and consult a board for the resident's room numbers. I see my friends have hyphenated their last names to Peterson-Anderson.

The apartment is tiny, but after our truck house, it seems luxurious to have more than one room. It is furnished mostly with Import Warehouse wicker and a couple of wood screens from India. There are some mushrooms in a planter that look as though they were transplanted, with moss intact, from local woods.

Karen takes out a pot from the refrigerator and puts it on a stove burner. Jack sits down with a Havana cigar box and begins to roll a number of reefers. He brushes the seeds and stems to the side, choosing the best of his minced grass for the joints. I keep contrasting our generation of the sixties to my parents' era. Their idea of hospitality is to invite guests into an immaculate living room.

There are candles everywhere of every height. Electricity is used for overall illumination only until the matches are found.

Richard helps himself to the spaghetti while Jack lights the end of the rolled Zigzag papers. Taking a couple of sticks of incense, Karen puts them in holders perforated to hold them upright.

I'm the only one whose hands are still. For a minute of time the others are the participants, and I am an observer. I ask myself in my moment of watching if it is really all right now that we smoke some dope. Even my questioning surprises me. The joint is being passed now from Jack to Richard, who's already exhaling in anticipation of filling his lungs to the maximum with smoke. He'll hand it to Karen, who will give it to me.

I feel tired of examining ethics in even this small deed. No one wants the ghost of the calorie counter to whisper a high number when the fudge cake is being sliced.

"Me, next, Richard," I say, to cut in front of Karen and banish this wisp of wondering.

While following into infinity the silver line of incense smoke, I'm imagining if the alphabet had fifty letters what their shapes and sounds would be. It's Richard who interrupts us in our private reveries. He relates our selling of the house and all its contents. He speaks the fact like a simple headline, and Jack, after whistling once, asks to know the story.

"Laurel was reading the Scriptures." I stand up at this cue to find my Bible, feeling a little like Alice in Wonderland, who ate some portion on a table and grew to fill the room. Looking for the pages with all the words in red, I begin to read aloud. Richard actually falls asleep while Jack and Karen listen, staring, heads together, into each other's eyes.

"Hey, you guys. I always thought there were only twelve disciples. Listen to this. There was a huge group, men and women, who followed around with Jesus."

I look up and find both Peterson-Andersons asleep now too. It's my job to cover everyone and later blow out all the candles.

January 19

The sound of the rain begins to rouse me; it's beating against the window glass. The pillows that I pushed together to create a bed have separated under my weight through the night.

My sense of smell follows behind the sound of the howling weather. Pancakes are unmistakably being turned on a griddle. Reluctantly I open my eyes. My lean husband, in Levi's, is standing with a coffee cup in the kitchen doorway. His hair is longer now than when we met, curling up his neck just above the collar of his favorite army shirt. His fervor for military surplus stores is almost patriotic. It is certain that we will buy drab green packs, sleeping bags, and coats with a chest full of military pockets. By tomorrow we'll be on some on ramp soliciting rides to a more temperate climate.

Sitting up, I can now see Jack punctuating whatever he's saying with his hands. I turn from them to reach under my shirt and fasten the hooks on my bra. The rest of dressing is to find my shoes and press my pants' waistband snaps together.

"Look," says Jack to my husband. "LSD is tasteless, odorless, and transparent. Imagine the effect it would have if it could be dropped into public water systems. It could bring enlightenment to a nation."

"Or insanity," I interject while helping myself to a pancake from the frying pan.

Jack laughs. There's the hoot of a bird in his tone, and he even flaps his elbows. He brings up a new topic, the validity of UFOs, and how the government is suppressing all information to prevent panic.

I think of it as drug talk. There are numbers of topics born in the curl of marijuana smoke, just as drug art has a distinct form of repetitive lines.

Going back to the living room I choose to look outside at the streaming rain rather than interact. I'm sure now that the real process of aging is internal, and not, as supposed, in the wrinkling of the skin.

January 21

We look like the invasion of the green sea blobs. I'm behind Richard, who is also wearing an army-issue rain parka. With them blossoming over our packs we are three-hundred-pound creatures trudging through mud at the roadside. The drawstring hood is cutting off some of my range of vision, leaving only my nose to be clearly exposed to those passing by. Between us is Noah on his new leash.

Almost to the California border, our rides have only been for relatively short distances between off ramps. My discomfort then was in being forced to sit on the edge of the seats because of my pack's protrusion under this voluminous plastic slicker. The cars have had warm heaters running too, and I imagined each time that I had olive green sweat beginning to moisten my pores.

Cranking my head to look up at my husband, I'm sorry that speech is almost impossible. My mouth is muffled by my coat's collar. I would like to express my hope to reach the edge of clouds, to step past some line in nature and have a shadow again beneath our feet. I'm tired of the infinite varieties of rain, from mist or drenching, that we've experienced since leaving Portland.

An old station wagon pulls to the shoulder ahead. Running up to its door I can see hundreds of small dents along its frame as if it once passed through a meteor storm. The driver is somewhere between forty and sixty. A two-day stubble along his chin is accentuated by the stark, black coat he's wearing.

"There's no heat in here, kids. Going to Frisco if this car will make it."

We put both our packs and ponchos, with the puppy, in the back. There're also a couple of tires and an old Samsonite suitcase that looks like it has suffered from cigarette burns.

"Bought this in Seattle. Terrible on gas and cold in here, but it beats walking."

Our driver laughs as if his dialogue has been the punch line of a colossal joke. Climbing in the backseat, I let Richard have the front. I'm already calculating that San Francisco by tonight will only be a short distance to my parents' house across the bay.

"We've got a radio, though, which is something." Our driver snaps it on, and static fills the car that's loud enough to make our dog bark. After twisting down the volume knob, he turns the channel selector. A rich voice booms forth with tones that suggest English farms and pails of fresh milk.

"And all the prophets from Samuel, and those that follow after, as many as have spoken, have likewise foretold of these days. You are the children of the prophets, and of the covenant which God made with our fathers . . ."

93

Our driver, determining the program to be of religious content, turns the selector knob to moaning music of lost love. Only the manners of a hitchhiking guest keep me from crying aloud. I want to hear more. It's as though I'm exhausted and here there are box-spring words where I can rest. After the song's last drum-accompanied whine, our driver snaps it off. He has offered it to us only as proof of a functioning radio.

"I'm Roy," he says to Richard, taking one hand off the wheel in greeting.

"Once this open road gets in your blood, boy, you can't help but be a drifter like me. Nothing can hold you; may get a wife, and even a kid, bit it's the highway you love."

I shudder at the thought that any of his words will lodge like a curse within Richard. As Roy continues with elementary instruction on how, if riding rails, to jump off before hitting the freight yards, I feel uncomfortable. He's tapped my tiny seed of fear that my husband would rather move on than stick with anything.

I make myself rest after crossing the state line. After awhile, I haul my knapsack up to use as a pillow.

We're approaching the six Nimitz Freeway exits providing access to Fremont. I could have called my parents' 797-prefix number when Roy left us in the city, again in Hayward, and now at a gas station just miles from their house. I refuse because it would mean asking for help simultaneous with announcing our arrival. Now I'm in the front seat instructing our salesman host exactly where to drop us.

Collecting our gear, we walk up an incline and along a sidewalk bordering a modern movie house with a choice of six screens. There's a legion of memories here that I'm too tired to translate for Richard. I once ran away and cut through that field with rabbits darting around me. Now, it lies under the concrete of a chain-store mall. With the intersection's green light we cross a double-width street to the shoreline of suburban housing. We are one right angle turn from Richmond Avenue and four blocks to my parents' corner. There's no fatigue in me now, but a familiar combination of anticipation and apprehension.

Sometimes I've perceived my parents during visits as beings with two distinct heads. The first face is genuine with welcome, but in time can weary in its place of dominance and let the second head swivel to the front. The second, with pointed teeth, is verbal with chiding disapproval.

I recite to myself all the neighbors' names, substituting the proper nouns to fit an old poem that invokes the bells of London town:

> Oranges and lemons
> Toll the bells of the O'Maras.
> Pancakes and fritters
> Say the bells of the Mattsons . . .

We cross the grass to the front door with its three panes of rippled glass that no one can see through. My mother covers the little windows every year with wrapping paper to decorate the porch for Christmas. Hearing the television, I know from memories of a thousand days it's the local night news. I ring the bell and also knock. My fathers footsteps approach, and his voice questions before he'll touch the door, "Who's there?"

"It's me, your daughter!"

"Pat," he cries, "Laurel's here!"

By instruction our boots are abandoned outside; the dog goes in the backyard; and we sit at the breakfast room table, sock-footed, eating split pea soup.

"Yes, sir, to answer your question, we decided to postpone Alaska for the spring," replies Richard.

He's chosen the smallest square of facts to hang out on the conversation line. The bulk of the details are going to stay wadded inside.

I study my parents sitting across from us smiling and know they are most receptive now to the truth of our conversion experience.

"I've got something to tell you that really has changed our

lives." Seeing my father exchange a fast glance with my mom, I have to smother a laugh. They think I'm going to announce a pregnancy.

"We have both made a commitment to follow Christ."

I can read the almost imperceptible movement at the corner of lips, a further depression of cheek, a slight narrowing of the eye. It clearly translates their exasperation. Within myself I acknowledge they have the right to the thought "What next?" I've sat before in this very chair on visits from Berkeley to explain that I'm giving up meat, and much earlier even suggested that we chew heavenly blue morning glory seeds together. That time they confiscated my psychedelic guidebook and threw me out of the house.

"Dad, think of everything before as me knocking on hollow doors."

Mother interrupts with instructions for where we can sleep. "Sounds good," says Richard as he stands up. I ask if we can go as a family to church in the morning. I can hear my father exhale one short breath. For years now they have limited their attendance to sometimes at Easter.

"We can do that, Jim," says my mother.

I sense both her and Richard with trowels in their hands ready to smooth any rough cement.

After taking the bowls to the sink, I go to get my pack from the hall. Our canvas frames are leaning against a small bookcase filled with the *Encyclopedia Britannica*. Directly above it are two framed high-school photos of my sister and me in formal gowns. I remember how old I felt wearing mascara, and having my hair teased at a beauty shop into a bouffant flip. Now, to that girl in her green satin, I'm a married woman and have finally grown up.

I have to laugh at myself going down the hall. That same self-image of maturity is perpetuating itself like a mirage. I'm full of illusions. The truth is I want to become truly mature. I take the thought and hoist it up into my night's prayer.

FREMONT

January 22

The church parking lot has twice as much asphalt as needed to accommodate the small number of vehicles coming for morning service. Crossing from my father's car to the double doors, I'm sorry my mother wouldn't come. She spoke of "Sunday dinner" as if every letter were a capital that needed her alone to prop on the table.

We are handed a bulletin with a garden photo cover that has the full-color quality of calendar pictures. From the door greeter, who has her name on a plastic tag, we cross the vestibule to a man who has the word "Usher" pinned to his chest. We are seated near the back. It's almost eleven. The mahogany pews resemble the curving rib cage of an architectural creature. There are so few people in it that it could be in danger of becoming extinct. I wonder if it's full only on Easter.

Tiny whispers are hardly pitched above the rustle of clothing. Almost everyone has a head bent in what I think at first is prayer, but now see is the collective activity of bulletin reading. The left-hand page meticulously details the order of service, while the right side lists interchurch activities, including the address of the month's potluck. My father is already opening a rose-colored hymnal to mark the first song. Imitating him, I begin to turn to the designated page when strains of music announce the beginning of the service. There are no theatrical velvet curtains opening, but there's a feeling that something much like that has just occurred. As the organ chords subside the pastor rises to the pulpit center stage. He has a formal voice that enunciates every syllable. I dub his language choice to be a kind of "high manners" that purrs, "Thank you to the churchgoers for their timely attendance."

He reads the morning prayer, instead of speaking from his heart. In the wisp of a thought, I wish I had insisted on staying home to help my mother. Even the scripture, which I expected to crackle with reality, sounds dull in his mouth. Sunday dinner definitely could have used four preparing hands.

The offering plate is passed by an usher. It's a hardwood platter lined with purple felt. My father puts in a folded dollar, and Richard flips in some pocket change.

The message is a philosophical discourse on the value of the human being. One has to search in the shadows of his paragraphs to find the reference that we were created in the image of God. I discern that the gentleman in front of me has had difficulty staying awake. His head tips down to his right shoulder. The sermon is so boring that I envy his momentary loss of consciousness. I wonder if this message could be put on tapes and distributed as a safe, organic means of inducing sleep. It could be packaged as an alternative to sleeping pills.

Exact to the second hand sweeping up to the hour, the service is concluded with another written prayer.

Neither my father nor Richard have any interest in complimentary coffee announced as available in the fellowship hall. We ride down Glenmore Drive in silence. Like rearranging furniture, I keep reorganizing the service to somehow be more of a celebration than a duty.

"They should pass out harmonicas, kazoos, and even soda pop bottles with different levels of water so we could blow some living sounds. Request ten or more people to quote a favorite verse with an explanation why, so I could learn something."

Richard silences me with a look.

The table is set in the dining room. There's both a fruit and a lettuce salad. Richard remarks, while passing me the meat platter, that we'll be leaving in the morning. Intuitively, I guess that he would prefer to go as soon as we finish this meal. There's an invisible current of restlessness.

"We thought of going straight down to see my parents in Los Angeles, but I'm now considering routing us south through Nevada."

My parents make no comment, or are holding one back.

The Sunday paper has been shifted into piles along the couch and rug. I propose a walk to Richard after dinner to force exercise against the waves of dull reading and drowsiness.

Noah comes too, but without a leash. Only children and an occasional retired person seem to use the sidewalks in my parents' subdivision. All other legs walk to an automobile.

"That's the last time, Laurel, I'm going to church. It was utterly dull!"

Richard's tone is friendly and conversational, but I see his comment to be like a move of black checkers; and mine are the red that must jump over them.

"That's a ridiculous conclusion—to write off all the congregations in America because this one was particularly boring. Let's just keep looking."

"You can," is his reply. "Everything that really matters we've already learned by that experience of salvation."

Our conversation seems to be more like a tic-tac-toe game than checkers. No one can win. I perceive real Christianity to be like an immense house. I don't want to stop exploring just because we're through the narrow door.

Noah starts barking at a cat that is gliding between holly bushes and a house. It diverts our conversation, and I release the issue, hoping Richard is only reflecting the transitory sentiments of a weary Sunday afternoon.

NEVADA
January 26

I like most of the cheap hotels. Even though the price is rarely over six dollars and the bathrooms are always down the hall, each one is different. Carrying my pack down the stairs for another morning of desert hitchhiking, I admire the boxes of Indian arrowheads mounted on the wall. The artifacts were not arranged in rows, but elaborately laid in patterns like formal gardens of old stones. The stairs are unique too. There are dabs of silver meal rounding out each corner that would normally collect dust.

While looking down, I admire my new cowboy boots. Richard and I each got a ten-dollar pair. They feel as comfortable as a baby's bed for the first half of the day. By night, though, my feet cry to come out of them.

My husband has already gone outside with his pack and the dog. I pass the rocking chairs that flank a cage where we paid our money. The desert morning is already shimmering with million-mile vistas in every direction.

"The bakery's open."

My husband, waiting on the sidewalk with a white sack, hands me some wheat bread. I know the plan as I stand next to him and eat. As on our other mornings, we'll continue south. Today, by the map's lines, we should merge onto a main road with more traffic.

We fall into step, our gait as equal as walking bookends. The few houses, gas stations, and cafés are clustered together to make a stand for civilization against the barren landscape. No matter the gallons of water lavished on lawns and flower beds, it all looks precarious. The wind and elements could easily reclaim Little Burg, Nevada.

Feeling lighthearted, I find simple verses come easily to me, and I would rather sing my rhymes than talk. Richard wishes aloud for a harmonica, and then complains that he should have brought with us a little of Jack's stash. Using both hands, I pantomime rolling a giant joint of fresh air. After licking the invisible ends, I lift it up and suck in enormous amounts of healthy oxygen before gesturing to give it to my husband.

Only two cars pass, and the drivers keep their eyes averted

from our solicitations. While letting Noah off the leash, Richard picks up some rocks and challenges me to target practice with cactus.

"You know, we have less than fifty cents left, Laurel." Since we are neither hungry, thirsty, nor dirty, this news doesn't threaten my present moment, but I'm well aware how it will challenge a pending hour. It's like seeing the train tracks and knowing we are going to be tied to them. The locomotive of some need will come, and God will have to deliver us. My thought feels noble, but my mind is also furrowed with ditches that lack faith. It's out of that depression I speak.

"Well, we were dumb, then, to buy these boots. Twenty dollars could get us all the way to LA!"

"If these shoes pinch, you're right, but since they are utterly comfortable, you're wrong!"

While I laugh a vapor trail in the sky precedes the sound of a jet engine. I've stopped walking as I hear the news of our finances. I don't want to get too far away now from the little town, so we can return, if necessary, and use the free facilities of a service station.

Since neither of us owns a watch, we've become estimators of conventional time. We even substitute some aspect of the physical world to mark the hour. At the time that the first vision of mirage moisture appears on the tar highway, a speeding car brakes for us. It even runs partly off the shoulder and into the sand. I had been comparing the shadows of Joshua trees to find one wide enough for both of us to stand out of the sun and rest. Now, running with Richard, I think about a whole tin roof covering us—and maybe air-conditioning.

It's one of the varieties of Ford sedans. I see a couple in the front, and the fact that all the windows are open communicates there's no system forcing cooled air through vents. There are two doors, and the woman has to lean forward while pulling back the seat.

The rear always provides a view of profiles and the backs of heads. Our clean-shaven driver has on a cowboy hat. His companion has the kind of hair that's short and curled on top, while the rest hangs long with a wave, roller width, at the end.

"We're Mr. and Mrs. Johnson."

Because she giggles with her announcement our driver adds they have recently taken the vows of what, for both of them, is a second marriage. Between them is a Styrofoam cooler. We take the offered sodas and share the last of a box of Broasted chicken. We are now as dependent on God to eat as the wild creatures who own no cupboards.

The proximity of meat propels Noah up from the floor to beg. Tearing off some skin, I drop it into the cavern of our dog's mouth. We still have in Richard's pack over half a bag of puppy kibble.

"I'm Dotty, and this here is Sam."

I mumble back our first names, fascinated by the color spectrum that's been applied to her eyelids. Starting with the darkest blue, the colors change in subtle hue to a final rose. The eyebrow is a plucked and narrow upper frame. I know her fingertips and toenails must be equally groomed. I'm Miss Plain, and she's Miss Fancy.

Since they are going eventually east, Richard suggests a town where we can get out that's still hundreds of miles away. Now speeding, we ride through what I imagine are Western movie sets. Cattle drives and Indians are over every hill.

Once we are dropped off on the roadside again, my shoulders feel sensitive to the weight of my pack as I hoist it on. We walk past some trailer houses that look permanently rooted into desert suburbs. The smell of outdoor barbecuing seems to summon some demon who wants to list in my mind every possible food that can be grilled to succulence. Dragging myself along behind Richard I'm flooded with yearnings for a home. There's a need in me to put flowers on a table. I want to cut up old pillowcases into squares of cloth that can be embroidered with Bible verse fancies. There are supposed to be woods and moose outside my door.

Even while I'm listing the pillow and picture scraps that can turn bare walls into a home, a green-and-white squad car pulls up beside us at the curb. The length of the vehicle equals the exact length of the space that I've lagged behind my husband.

Richard inquires about camping facilities, or any place where we can lay our bags out for the night. The patrolman is young. There's some hesitation in his reply, "Nothing like that is available here. There's a city ordinance against hitchhiking wherever there's any housing or business."

I know what's ahead; we'll trek well off the road and make camp. All that I can think of, while shifting weight and trying to maintain a polite expression, is a Walt Disney movie: *The Living Desert* featured sidewinder snakes, scorpions, lizards, and fuzzy spiders.

"Well," he says, "there is one other place. No one is in our jail right now. It's been quiet for a long time, you can stay for a night."

I ask for a lift and climb first into the backseat. A metal mesh separates us from our driver. Looking straight ahead, I refuse to sneak a glance at Richard. The extensive radio equipment along the dashboard looks as though it could intercept the signals of Air Cuba.

A senior officer lays down a magazine as we are ushered into the facilities. Doing his best to suppress a grin, he's in complete agreement about us using the accommodations for one night.

Finally we are alone in a cell with the door wide open. There're two twin-sized beds mounted like shelves into the wall.

"I really don't like this at all," says Richard, opting to go out immediately and walk the dog.

I'm just happy to avoid being ground level with the night's reptiles. Taking my coat from my pack, I fold it into a pillow. I remember the last and only time I was in jail. It was in the early fifties with my mother. She was a Brownie Scout leader and took our troop on a field trip to both the fire and police stations. I remember asking then if the door could be opened so we could try the bed. My request was refused, and it remained, until now, a forgotten and ancient curiosity.

January 27

Opening my eyes, I'm inches from a drab stucco wall. The morning light reveals smudges and grime. Spots of paint, shades lighter than the rest, have been splashed over what I imagine were once penciled obscenities. There's still one small slogan even with the ripples of my sleeping bag. The P has been obliterated, leaving the message KILL THE IGS.

Once I sit up and slip on my coat, I'm hungry. While organizing our gear into packs, I remark to Richard that the state would have fed us breakfast if we were malefactors.

"Ha," he replies. "I would rather starve, and so would you, than have this door locked!" His voice is unusually heated; there's passion in his speech. Richard Lee has a past that I've asked him about and received only abrupt and partial answers. My husband once spent some nights in jail.

In single file we walk out, and I thank the officer on duty. I follow Richard, knowing we have a couple of miles to go before we can hitch. I'm fixated on something to eat. Looking into the glass windows of a café I glimpse the motion of syrup being poured over pancakes. Men press toast crusts into eggs fried over easy. A customer stands up, forsaking half a plate of hash browns.

I read something last night and try to coax the words out from dark memory into light. It's the poet apostle's alliteration, "abased and abound." "I have learned," he wrote, "in whatever state I am to be content."

The roadway is sand and dirt. One house got the city sidewalk, and the next one didn't. It's getting too hot to keep on my coat. Needing to stuff it in my pack, I dip my hands into the pocket thinking I may have left my comb in its folds. The lining has already torn inside, and I can run my fingers through a layer of government khaki clear around to my back. There's a coin partially buried in the stitching of an internal hem. "A quarter," I exclaim, holding it up. Since the money is meant to be spent, we quicken our pace. It's too small to bother turning back for a large grocery, but Richard gestures at a small store ahead. Surrounded by houses, it probably has higher prices just for being convenient.

I cross the street alone, leaving Richard with both packs. Surprisingly, there's a deli counter along a wall with a row of stainless steel bowls of salads and sandwich spreads. This is more than a shop that supplies forgotten loaves of bread.

From a refrigerator bin, I choose a pint of whole milk. It's both a food and a drink. Feeling it cold in my hands, I'm imagining the taste as I slide it to the cash register.

The clerk is wrapped against any flying food scraps in an encompassing white apron. She pushes a key that rings a machinery bell and asks for thirty cents.

"Not this time," I say, and move to put it back. All the cows could be on Jupiter for their proximity to me trying to get a drink. Offended by small-town Nevada inflation, I can't think of anything else I want. The warp of my disappointment is stubbornness; nothing within my budget looks good. I'll starve all day rather than take twenty-five pieces of gum with their Dubble-Bubble fortunes.

"Are you with them?"

I look back at the woman, who is motioning at the window. Richard is clearly visible. He's bending over stroking Noah. I affirm that's my husband with our dog.

"We might have a bone here," she says while moving toward a roll of butcher paper. I watch her wrap up what could be a small dinosaur's forearm. In addition she puts varieties of cheese and salami slices on another sheet. Getting bags, she adds some bread and napkins.

"Oh, pickles," she murmurs, and pulls two large ones out of a container to wrap in cellophane. She slides all the parcels across the counter: "Please keep that milk."

I thank her in awe. The retail value of her gift is but a few dollars, but the magnitude of her act can be valued only in gold.

On the back wall, behind my shop clerk, are some public notices tacked up with the deli menu. Among the papers, I see a calendar picturing Jesus in the midst of his disciples. I wave my way outside with a vigor that thoroughly exercises my wrist.

Richard stares, incredulous at the number of parcels balanced between my arms. I'm laughing and want to make up a science-fiction story about crossing a time warp into the 1880s. Then, bread was a few cents and a quarter bought a multitude of things.

I'm conscious that we are still in our patron's view. We could now both wave until our wrists ache. I could pull out a back sheet from my diary and record my taste buds bowing in gratitude. Instead, we walk out of sight.

We choose to sit where the desert is no longer behind fences, but now separates yards. Legally, we can hitch again. I lean back against my pack with the soft bread wrapped over a cheese slice. The more I satiate myself with food, the more casual I become about crusts and crumbs. Real hunger produces a dining alchemy; appetite turns common food into the fare of kings.

"We just need one good long-distance ride, and we could even get to LA."

It all feels possible. Our number is on the rolling dice, but there's no such thing as chance. Every roll now, I know is part of a plan.

LOS ANGELES
January 28

It's Richard's turn to reflect. I have few memories of Los Angeles. I float by my husband, exhausted from our last, long ride but feeling placid as a cloud. Let him recall the deeds of our lives; my history here is limited to us pulling in this morning, and our days in Venice.

We're walking down another main boulevard lined with palm trees. All the streets look much the same, but Richard assures me that this one will connect with the freeway to Newhall where his parents live. Layers of haze mute the distant mountains. I wonder if the local weather report runs figures for air pollution along with the temperature's highs and lows. It's a modern fact of LA along with the daily tides and the phases of the moon.

"See, what did I tell you?"

Richard, while restraining Noah, points at an on ramp that has a line of cars waiting to see their speedometers escalate from 0 to 65. A special traffic signal regulates the flow with a red light that turns green at thirty-second intervals. I feel that we, raising our thumbs to hitch, have somehow taken on the role of the missing yellow light: "Caution, prepare for change. For us you'll accelerate or stop."

A car behind us honks, and the driver motions for us to board with him. The vehicle's right front has been smashed in what must have been a major accident. The automobile is also such a dull gray it's not paint at all but some chemical coating preliminary to color. We have to move quickly with the imposed rhythm of merging traffic.

"I'm Jim." He is bearded with electric chin whiskers curling like tiny springs.

"What's your sign?"

Berkeley has schooled me for that question, but instead of naming my birth month's configuration of stars, I would rather credit God, who created the constellations. Giving our names, I make it clear we're not into astrology anymore.

"So you're a couple more of those Jesus freaks."

Unknowingly, he has tapped a need within me.

"Where have you met them?" I ask, thinking I have to meet others that have truly experienced salvation. Every generation must have its creatures that really make it to the ark.

"Ah," says Jim. "They're turning up everywhere. One of the biggest grass dealers in LA has thrown away his stuff. Now, that's crazy!"

"Where did he throw it?" asks Richard with a laugh.

The flowing traffic that I anticipated is instead a solid sludge of creeping vehicles. Both directions are affected, and I know it's not an accident that has caused such blockage but millions of people sharing the same road.

"Damn," says Jim. "I usually avoid rush hour." Turning in his seat, he asks, "What do you do for work?"

The question is for Richard, who answers that he does a little of everything without even glancing at our driver. His unvarying stare at the bumpers ahead seems like a symptom of "pre--parent visit" tension.

The traffic thins as we climb into the hills. Full color billboards advertise future housing projects. Richard gives instructions where to drop us on the road shoulder. Having pack-sore shoulders I want to suggest that we should phone the Lees, but I remember that I didn't want to bother my own parents.

We walk in silent compatibility. The land, with its sunburned grass, is endangered. The soil is about to be covered with wall-to-wall carpeting and cement patios. In the valley below us is the retirement community where Richard's family lives. The golf course looks like the center of some lopsided, modern flower blooming on the vine of a highway. The rooftops are its rectangular petals.

We descend, and I too feel anxiety. I met Bart and Ruby briefly in the role of their son's girlfriend, and now I'm a wife.

Almost in their door Richard smooths some wrinkles from the front of his shirt. Because of my carelessness we have only one remaining comb, which we pass between each other. Richard's last act, before knocking, is to pocket it as owner and custodian.

"Why, Bart," shouts Mrs. Lee, "Richard's here. I thought it was the cleaning lady coming early."

"I'm the lady that needs a cleaning," is my single thought as I follow my husband through the door.

"How about a kiss?" Ruby asks her stepson, and then notices our boots and our dog.

We are instructed to retreat first and deposit our shoes, packs, and pet back outside. Ruby explains it's the rug: "Don't ever get a white carpet for your home. I'm its slave!"

Complete exhaustion lets me imagine the rug rising up, drawing in from all the corners to an imposing height, and its wooly voice dictating what it allows to tread on its pile.

Bart Lee comes out in a bathrobe to shake his son's hand.

"We thought you kids were on the way to Alaska."

Ruby adds that there's not much on hand to eat. "Will you be here overnight?" she asks. "You should see my address book. I've already crossed out your Venice address, and Portland."

Richard inserts that we'll probably stay just one night. I follow my mother-in-law and husband through the breakfast room to the den. She instructs us how to pull out the couch in there to make a bed. She's sorry now that they picked this floor plan with its one bedroom. While she's talking, I take a handful of peanuts from an open can on a portable TV tray.

"Now, make yourselves some toast, and there is some cereal. We'll be done with our bathroom that has the tub in just a few minutes."

To me the word *shower* rhymes with *bower,* and my desire is to bathe more than to eat. Yet, with Ruby retreating to their room at the other side of the house, I am the first in the kitchen.

There're several bottles of amber-colored alcohol pushed back against the wall on the little counter between the stove and refrigerator. Everything is in gleaming order, and as we were told, there isn't much in the refrigerator besides some covered leftovers and a loaf of sliced white bread. Richard wipes up the crumbs in between the sets of toast.

Bart Lee, now in a short-sleeved shirt, joins us. His hair has been recently shaved into such a radical crew cut that there's no length for texture, but just a dark and grizzled shading.

"You know, there are still a lot of relatives back in Fergus Falls, along with Grandma Gadbow. Anyway, here are some wedding gift checks that came in late, that we've been holding until we could get an address for you."

I fill a bowl with water for our dog. My concern about what we are going to do next has lifted. Maybe we can turn toward Alaska again, working our way north. Without even glancing at the amounts, Richard pockets the checks and offers me the first shower. He further suggests that we take a morning walk with Noah around the golf course.

"Okay, how much?" I'm squeezing the ends of my wet braid that's hanging down my back. "Don't make me guess."

Richard feigns a surprised look and nods at an older woman with violet white hair who passes us. She tugs the leash to keep her Pomeranian moving, which has stopped to smell our dog.

"Seventy-five dollars, total," Richard replies, after assessing that I'm not in the right humor to be playfully delayed.

"Fabulous," I cry, knowing that amount, with good rides, can take us clear into Canada.

"I have a plan," says Richard. "Isn't the sun wonderful? I'm not in any hurry to get wet and cold right away. The rest of the world is still in winter. Let's take this money into Mexico and buy maybe a kilo of marijuana, which could be sold for enough profit to almost finance our Alaska journey."

His idea strikes me as wild. There's too much risk, and it violates my ethics. We can't earn our money for our homestead by breaking the law and living with that kind of tension.

I'm sorry we even stopped at Jack and Karen's after selling our truck. Richard did some dope that night, and that little taste has been fanned to the point where he has to have more.

I look over at my husband, who is staring at a party of men in pastel shirts playing golf. He seems to me so compulsive. In wanting to be close to God, he sells everything, and now desiring grass, he wants to buy a giant bag.

"It just isn't right, Richard!"

"Show me where it says in the Bible you can't smoke marijuana. You're not the only one reading it, Laurel. It says somewhere, 'Everything is lawful,' and before that, 'He didn't quench the burning flax.' "

"Those are just parts of verses. It's like picking the one bead or the fragment that matches what you want and ignoring all the rest on the string."

"What about that epistle you once quoted, 'That now there is no condemnation . . .' "

I feel as though I'm back in time fighting with my sister. I hated for her to rub her socks together, and every time I came into the room she would purposely grate her white nylon feet together, until I hit her and would then be the one in trouble. My overwhelming impulse is to make a fist and punch my husband.

"Okay, Richard," using my voice that's rusted through with sarcasm. "So now we bend the Bible, where before we wanted the Scriptures to bend us."

We walk in a stormy silence. Our feet are slapping down upon the pavement harder than necessary.

"It's your decision, Laurel. I'm going into Mexico, and you can come with me, or not. You can go wait in Fremont then."

I'm immediately sad. This is the most serious altercation we have ever had. Maybe our exhaustion is creating short circuits in our logic.

In a soft voice I ask about our dog. An animal without a veterinarian's certification would not be allowed to cross the border.

Richard replies that he has a good friend in the valley who has a fenced backyard. "Look, Noah will have a rubber ball and a tree, and will live awhile without a leash."

We both know he's won. The tug of war for the direction of the compass needle is over now.

As Richard turns back toward the house, he takes my arm and estimates the traveling time to San Diego. "Then, Tijuana, Laurel, is such a short distance. We'll change dollars to pesos and take a bus farther into the interior."

I shrug my shoulders. I guess it's not my job to try and be a conscience. I consider that role to be much like the cleaning woman of the heart. I've got my own dirty spots that need scrubbing before trying to disinfect my husband.

TIJUANA
February 1

The border is nothing but a line. Yet for those on this side it means small children selling Chiclet packages in the street.

Looking up at the makeshift houses that cover the Tijuana hills, I know there is like poverty in America but tucked behind prosperity's curtain. Here, the enterprises of survival are center stage.

We have passed what must be a thousand vendors. Besides the plaster statues and oil paintings on velvet are carts of food. Corn on the cob, rolled in red spice, is skewered on raw sticks and handed to customers. Enormous glass jugs are filled with juices.

I keep lagging behind Richard, who turns twice per block asking for me to keep abreast. His tone is without censure. I'm obviously enjoying myself, which further votes for his being right about our direction. Trying to find the bus for the central station, we've been walking by commercial automobile repair businesses. Every yard seems to have a bone pile of machinery parts. I have to skirt the rib cage of a radiator, and we veer around some old tires on the walkway.

"I've only seen one thing that I would really like to buy, Richard. A woman, back by the border had a pile of embroidered blouses over her arm."

"Maybe later," he says. "I think, Laurel, we would be really smart to deal with an American when we buy the grass. I don't mind paying a little more to be safe."

I see that my husband's mind is just chewing the gum of his plan. I refrain from correcting his phrase from the plural "we" to "you" buy. Yet he's introduced the topic, and I have some questions.

"It's easy to get into Mexico, but how do you propose carrying out a kilo? Everyone walks by an inspection guard. He sends any that feel suspicious to a second inspection. Maybe there are dogs trained to smell your *Cannabis sativa*."

Richard is absolutely quiet. I strike again.

"The law will treat you as if your destination were a grammar school and your intent to sell reefers by the swing set."

I can feel the terror I've induced. It compares to describing an IRS audit to a businessman without receipts to match his deductions.

Richard's reply is a soft monotone hum, which is interpreted to mean, "I'm thinking." Feeling suddenly lighthearted I have to suppress a laugh and to refrain from asking about prison food. I'm sure he's abandoned his idea of smuggling. I recite, out of relief, what I can remember of the pledge of allegiance in Spanish. Language was once my first-period class in high school, and every day I had to put my hand over my heart and quote, "*Juro fideliadad . . .*"

The local bus looks so rugged that Timex should attach watches to its frame to prove they are still running after any twenty-four-hour shift. The driver has put a small plastic statue of Mary on the dashboard. Pictures of saints and plastic roses stick out of both visors. He has also wrapped his steering wheel and gearshift with three colors of tape. We pay our pennies, and more crowds board. Richard stands up for a woman who has bundles and a baby all held under, and in the folds of, a black shawl.

The central terminal is a roof over a number of different bus lines. In the entrance is a man who has a canary cage resting on a striped pole. In his hand he offers boxes filled with tiny fortune slips. Upon payment the bird will extract one at random to be read.

Two different carriers advertise regular departures to Mazatlán as one of the cities served along their route to Mexico City. Richard calculates that, without delays, it will be a twenty-seven-hour journey ahead. We choose the company whose name translates as Three Stars of Gold, which has an immediate departure.

There's more crowding at the gate than any forming of a line. A lot of the passengers have created suitcases by wrapping ropes around boxes and tying special knots for handles. Everyone is guaranteed a seat, but so far there is no driver in sight.

"I'm going to run and buy us a soda. If you can board before I'm back, Laurel, try for a seat in the front so we can have the extra visibility through the windshield."

The driver comes in a uniform that looks like it was borrowed from an aviation museum exhibit of old pilot's clothes. I sling my backpack over the rail to the front seat before sliding in. My husband is outside, at the back of the line, holding up to me two plastic bags filled with Coke.

Finally aboard, Richard hands me mine, which is drawn precariously up around a straw. He explains that it's assumed one would rather have this packaging than pay the extra deposit for bottles. The bus seats have the capacity to recline for three inches, yet I know the journey will be uncomfortable and exhausting. It's going to be like being jostled between the folds of a giant *National Geographic* magazine.

Once we're under way the evening color silhouettes the desert cactus and an occasional village.

"Laurel, I've thought of a safe alternative. We could mail the grass into the States. Look, it would be wrapped in small amounts so as not to make one suspicious box. If any is intercepted, we would still be able to claim most of it."

Hearing my husband enthusiastically voice this new plan, I feel that I've been translated from the light side of the moon to the dark. Even my window view has altered; from a charming street scene of vendors using lanterns, it's now a depressing look at a poverty-level economy.

"I don't think it would work."

"Sure, it would. I'll send it to people like Jack and Triple. I'll use their right address, but change their names to a Spanish equivalent. If, somehow, there were an investigation, none of them would know anything. No one in Oregon even knows of our trip into Mexico."

I ask about the kinds of food served in jail, but he is deaf.

At the Mexicali depot some passengers depart, and new ones board. The bus will now leave the line of border and turn toward Hermosillo, which will be the first stop in the interior.

Instead of choosing my husband's shoulder, I lean against the window glass. Nothing is visible now. We have been traveling for some time through an uninhabited desert region. My window seems to mirror us. I feel that the invisible soul of what we are is heading into its own night and wilderness. I don't want to go back to that state of marijuana dependency. It seems now to be both seductive and deceiving. We need help. If God is looking over our shoulder, I ask all these thoughts to be changed into prayer.

MAZATLÁN
February 3

Once released from the jaws and gullet of the bus, we stroll along a walkway that borders the sea. There's been rain. The depressions and sidewalk cracks are filled with fresh water. My exhaustion makes me feel as though sand has sifted into me. Through this dullness I watch flocks of gray pelicans ride the distant breakers. My legs are taking inventory of every moving joint.

"Let's eat!" Richard points to a collection of plywood stands erected along the beach. All but the first one is boarded up. We sit on stools along a plank counter. From the sign for the menu I can interpret the word for "fish" but am unable to translate the varieties. Using the number of pesos as a guide, we point at our choice.

"Should we look next for a hotel?"

Richard never answers my question, because our plates are being placed in front of us. Somehow we have two different items. He has large fish chunks fried in a crispy batter, while mine is four baby swordfish, whose distinguishing lips protrude past the edge of my plate.

"Hotel," I repeat.

"No, what I've heard is about these trailer parks located beyond those beach high rises. They are designed for tourists and should have good camping facilities. Let's check that out first."

After settling our bill, we resume walking in the direction Richard indicated. A blue city bus passes us by. Its painted number is the same as others that have been traveling by us at about fifteen-minute intervals.

"I'm afraid we're going to have to flag the next one down, Laurel. It could be a long walk to find the beach that's beyond all that construction."

Dutifully I nod, even though the thought of boarding another public vehicle is like contemplating the noise of fingernails scratching blackboards. I feel I'm losing the part of myself that's assertive. I have that same powerless feeling that tiny children do. They ride along in cars filled with their parents' cigarette smoke and never quite know the destination.

"Richard, how do you know there's a trailer park down here?"

"I don't."

Oh, we are both in the smoky backseat.

We climb aboard the next bus with a number of people wearing the uniforms of hotel employees. My husband, in the midst of people paying their fare, asks me for the Spanish words for "where," "trailer," and "park." Even though it would be more expedient to talk with me, the driver doesn't turn his attention from Richard. Directions are a man's business.

The reply is *"Si, olé,"* which Richard also understands, "Yes, hooray!"

We sit near the driver, puzzled by his response. The man across from us has stacks of tiny cages filled with crickets. He's talking to them in the tones of endearment used for pets.

I try to think about facts to keep from ending up as the next guest at the Mad Hatter's tea party. I am twenty-one. I have been married a little over three months. We are supposed to be on our way to Alaska to homestead.

Most of the hotels we pass are skeletal, in the process of being framed. Even though it is mid-morning the gray clouds, which were hanging over the water when we arrived, have rolled in and covered the sky. It looks like rain, and I hope we can find shelter, even if it's going to be our tent.

The driver hoots for our attention and smiles. His teeth are framed with silver. He's gesturing to the roadside. I read, "Olé Trailer Park and Camping Grounds." It's all hand-lettered in English above the logo of a sombrero perched on a limb of a cactus.

Richard strides to the office while I follow, surveying the accommodations. There are rows of individual sites each with its own thatched roof built over a picnic table. A number of Airstreams and other sleek trailers have taken the places closest to the water. At the end of the row of trailers is one umbrella tent erected alongside a Volkswagen van. A couple of gardeners are tending plants by what I assume are the Olé guest bathrooms.

The office is roomy and has a schedule of fees posted on the wall. For tents it is twenty-five dollars a month or ten dollars a week. Richard pays the seven-day minimum. A parrot without a cage swings on a perch inside an auxiliary room full of racks of bottled water.

"Real storm coming," says the owner in perfect English after he's put our bills in his wallet.

"Gale winds are being forecast." He gives some further instructions. We should camp in the back; some of trailers might have to move if the water level is going to rise with the turbulent ocean.

Once outside Richard asks me if there's a set number of miles per hour that constitutes a gale. I reply that I have no idea and look up at the glowering skies. Not at all fearful, I'm excited at the idea of "tropical adventure." This stimulant has temporarily absorbed all feelings of exhaustion.

We take the extra measures of fastening a rope to our tent besides using every ground stake. Richard thinks we should dig a small trench to collect any runoff of rain and prevent it from collecting under the tarp floor. He begins to use a large seashell that was abandoned at our spot. Behind us are palm trees amidst dense vegetation. There's a glimmer of a lake also shining through the distant, lush growth.

"Have you heard there's a hurricane coming? We're pulling out."

Richard and I look up at a man who's got shoulder-length brown hair pulled back into a ponytail low on his neck.

"We're in that van," he indicates, introducing himself as Arthur from Topanga.

"My friend and I have been living here this past month, but storm or no storm, it's time for us to go back."

Arthur starts to tell us how we can buy fillets of fresh fish by waiting at a particular point for the fishermen to return in the afternoon. "No one has been out these past two days. Listen to those breakers."

The sea does produce a constant roar.

"Why don't you come on over? We've still got some hot tea. We always like those who drop out, to drop in." He titters. "I can't believe you really took the bus from Tijuana."

We finish digging our small trench with the clamshell. After hearing the word "hurricane," I wonder if our trench is as absurd as filling a bucket of water in anticipation of a forest fire burning toward us.

"Richard, I'm just too tired to meet anyone. If they're getting ready to leave, maybe they really don't want company either."

"I'll be sensitive to that," he says, leaving me with both packs to pull through the tent flaps.

I remove my shoes and pull out my mummy sleeping bag. The pocket of it isn't wide enough to really turn within its quilted folds; it turns with me. Hearing the surf I think of a sea creature pulling me slowly into some dark cave of sleep.

Richard crawls by me. I say nothing, not wanting to puncture my rest and be back on that dry shore of interaction. I can hear rustling; his bag is unfolding.

It's dark, and I have to go to the bathroom. The issue of relieving myself was the business of my dream, but the pressure persisted until I woke. My husband is uttering the long, drawn breaths of someone far from consciousness. I feel around for my boots and crawl out holding them in my hand. Disoriented, I try to remember the direction of the toilets.

There's a line of trailers by the sea. Arthur's van is gone. There's neither moon nor stars as I make my way. The air feels full of moisture.

I look disheveled in the mirror's reflection. My hair has tangles from near my scalp to the ends halfway down my back. It has become twisted in my coat that I've been wadding up into a pillow. The wind has confirmed every knot.

I'm wide awake, and once outside I feel a beauty in the night. I seem like the only custodian awake to see its art. Back by our tent, I wish we had purchased a hammock even more than I once wanted the embroidered top. I decided to sit at the picnic table and untangle my hair.

Creeping by Richard, I seek the comb. It is in his Levi's, which will be folded and deposited at the top of his pack. Marriage is the learning of someone else's habits. Respectful of his sleep, I'm quiet untying the top cord. There's no folded denim, but a stiff plastic. Rubbing my hand over its surface, I can feel a large compressed brick of marijuana. I know he must have bought it from our fleeing neighbor, Arthur.

One of the reasons I hate it is that I'll have to live with temptation. Closing the pack back up, I decide that one shouldn't store chocolates at the fat woman's house. I'll want to smoke it. I like to share everything with my husband, and someday I'll surely laugh that I even worried whether it was good for us. Then it will be too late for the highest form of sanity, which is to stay straight.

I back my way outside again, now deeply disturbed. The sound of the waves is overpowering. I want to walk to the shore. Just as on my first night on the bus, I feel that nature is reflecting my mood. Then it was the darkness I felt was threatening us; now it is the coming storm. The sound leads me. I could be completely blind and still find the sea.

Why do I like getting high? The infinity of the night draws forth the question. Grass seems to ease things; pressures lessen, moods lighten. Smoking a joint always feels good, like taking off my shoes.

But then, I'm really choosing to walk no farther.

Suddenly weary with analysis, I turn back toward bed.

February 4

Because it's warm the driving rain is completely different than in Portland. It sounds like locust plagues wanting to devour our tent, and the world. We wake together—his movement, then mine, his whisper, my reply.

There's some water inside. The salesman should have said,

"*Mostly* or *almost* waterproof." The dripping is from a seam at the roof. We are quick now to gather up our sleeping bags.

"If this gets any worse, tonight I'm sure they'll let us put our bags in the office," says Richard.

"You can have the place under the parrot." My reply rides on the back of a laugh. The ground glistens with water. Most of the trailers have moved to a line behind the office. One of the gardeners is motioning to a driver backing up an enormous rig.

"I wonder," says Richard, "if all that is really necessary or if it's just to add to the drama of 'the coming storm.' "

There's no standing in contemplation of things; we take our packs and run toward the office. A number of people are milling around inside, sipping coffee from Styrofoam cups. Just as paper clothes are cut to fit cardboard dolls, these people exactly match the trailers. They have all the tabs of Americans in the retirement age bracket.

The room is full of the droning of English. One can smell the moisture evaporating into the warm, enclosed space. The men are wearing after-shave lotion. In that first flicker of people looking at us I contrast the curiosity we feel from Mexicans with the judgment of disapproval here. Olé Park is a small town, and everyone knows that we must be the occupants of the army tent. I'm sure their thought is now that Arthur's left, we have come. It makes me aware there are tangles in my hair.

Two or three start to talk to us as we lean our packs against the wall.

"Have you heard there's a hurricane schedule to hit this afternoon? The Mazatlán schools were closed first thing this morning and the children sent home."

"Surely it's not too late to get into town and back," I remark.

"No way you can," says a man in a blue nylon jacket. "All the public buses have been shut down. The telephones are out. José and Adono can't even leave for their own homes."

I'm now aware this means we have no access to any market. Our first business of today was to buy a quantity of food.

"That's your tent," says a man with an open beer can. "Better get it down, or you're going to lose it. Right here, on the beach, the wind gusts will tear out anything like that."

Our amusement at their preparations is replaced with concern. Richard looks at me; I can read the tension by the set of his mouth. Without hesitation we turn to rescue our belongings.

Influenced by the details that I've just heard, I now perceive the storm as malicious. We run, and the mud sucks at our boots. What yesterday was a glimmer of a lake is now a clearly visible body of water.

The stakes pull right out of the mud, and I deposit them in a plastic sack. We take the tent sides next, reducing its bulk by folding angles. Our movements are as much a ritual as the stowing of a flag at sunset. Too wet for the stuff bag, the tent is carried in Richard's arms as we run back to the office.

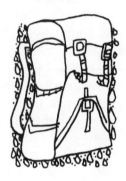

A woman shouts for me to shut the door. Her tone almost makes me want to retreat outside again. The storm can only blow upon me, whereas prejudice chills that which is within.

I'm irritable and pin my excuse on hunger. Not wanting to talk, I avoid eye contact by rummaging through my pack for a dry change of clothes. I'm aware of our tent dripping on the tile floor. Richard is standing next to me without the freedom to even open his bag for fear of revealing the marijuana. I make my way to the one bathroom, in the room with the blue water bottles. The parrot is gone. Maybe the owner carries him home at night on his shoulder. My eye surveys the shelves wishing for a package of crackers amidst the cleaning supplies and rolls of toilet paper.

"Poor Polly, there's nothing," I mutter.

Both the gardeners are waiting for me to come out, as well as Richard. They are all standing around the door clutching changes of clothes. The office has also emptied of most of the trailer owners. The women who were playing cards are gone, as well as the men with their coffee and beer.

It's an austere room. With the exception of one ashtray, the counter is bare. The white cement-block walls are without any adornment other than the placard of fees and a calendar featuring February. It's all a quiet counterpoint to the two windows that reveal the ferocious storm.

The man in the blue jacket stands staring outside. "I'm surprised the electricity has lasted this long," he comments.

Thinking of the supply shelves, I don't remember a single candle for the dark.

"Those poor people," he says, now turning so his back is completely to me.

I'm stricken. My whole concern has been the welfare of Laurel Lee. I'm safe, while outside are neighborhoods built of packing crates and paper. They are surely being destroyed in this deluge, along with livestock and crops.

All my criticisms of the trailer owners now accuse me. I've charged those faces with disapproving of us, the hippies, but really I exceeded them all in my attitude toward them. I have made no friends, because I have not showed myself to be friendly.

"I want to thank you for your counsel when we first came in this morning."

"Bob Shaw is the name."

This man now looks like someone who has pictures of grandchildren in his wallet. Maybe he's donated money all his life to help crippled children.

"We'll see that you get some dinner in here. It could be a long

125

night. My wife and I come every winter to Mazatlán. It will probably be clear and beautiful tomorrow."

As he leaves I sit back with my diary, looking up often to check the wind and listen to the roar of the water.

Richard sits next to me on the couch. "I haven't had time to tell you about yesterday," he confides.

The gardeners have come out too. They are both wearing borrowed clothes. Both their pants legs and shirt cuffs are rolled.

"Arthur's a dealer in Topanga and also a musician at someplace called The Bent Oak. He had several kilos, of which he was glad to sell me a compressed, uncleaned block."

I don't even want to look at Richard and watch his face forming all these words. I would rather he be a leader encouraging people to overcome their habits.

"Arthur was telling me how different it is in the East. We buy lids— right?—on the West Coast. In New York the equivalent is to ask for an ounce. Laurel, it can sell there for as high as fifty dollars. That same exact amount only fetches ten in Berkeley and the Haight."

Looking out at the trees through veils of rain, I can see that it's likely that some will be uprooted by morning.

"You have got to try this stuff. My pack is in that water room. I'll go roll us a joint. No one's here now, why not smoke it back there? There's a little window we can open in the bathroom."

When I first met Richard I used to exhale by quoting the Beatles, "We all live in a yellow submarine." Then, I would hold the golden wheat straw papers to my lips and submerge my lungs. But I can't anymore.

I am surprised at myself. I expected to struggle against an overpowering desire to get loaded. This strength can't be originating with me. The yearning for drugs is gone.

"No, Richard, I'm not going to, and I don't want to ever smoke dope again."

He is silent. Across from us José and Adono converse intently. On each side of the room our foreign languages make perfect privacy for all confessions and vows.

Richard stands up. I can tell that he's hurt. He turns to watch the storm while I stare at his handsome profile. His hair is curling up on the back of his neck. I want to touch his neck and shoulders. My thought is of how much I love him: "Please come in my direction." Growing is like a ladder between earth and heaven. It's lined with cunning books that can catch us and keep us from progress. Please keep climbing with me.

"Fine," he says. "Each to his own."

I watch him walk back to the storage room. Never before have I considered this tragedy in practicing religion. It has such potential to bring people to a perfect intimacy, but its paradox is that it can take them further apart. It introduces and endorses new standards. So that's the sword Jesus brought to earth!

Richard seems to be gone for a long time. There's a slight smell of burning grass, but more a pronounced draft from the open window. I can hear him take the mop from the bucket. The direction of the wind must have pushed a volume of rain through his open window.

I'm weak. I want to go back there to his arms and once I'm high take the mop and use it on the tiles like a giant brush. I'll do primitive paintings with storm water.

Mr. Shaw, now zipped from head to toe in a slicker, bustles through the door.

"We didn't have as much on hand as we thought," he apologizes. "But if you need anything more, ours is that second trailer on this side called Nomad."

With a wave he is gone, leaving a distant water trail where he walked over to leave his bag on the counter.

Adono and José help me pull out the food, and Richard comes out. They have given us a package of cooked hot dogs and buns. There are four apiece, plus boiled eggs and carrot sticks.

"No tortillas," says one of the gardeners in genuine dismay. Everyone laughs, and Richard puts his hand on my shoulder.

February 8

Three full days had to pass before Mr. Shaw was right about the weather. Mazatlán has been wet, gray, and littered with debris. Souvenirs of the storm, severed branches have covered the fields, and in town there are massive deposits of building scraps. My Spanish was too limited to comprehend the local newspaper's account of wind velocity and damages. Our distance from any news contributed to the feeling that we were just observers in Mexico, not participants.

Crawling out from the tent I have to squint against the sun. The shrimp fishermen are already casting their nets in the distant lagoon.

"The usual, please," says Richard behind me. We eat pineapples for breakfast. The juice drips down my arms, forcing me to try different positions in the hammock. Usually, I've been swimming in the morning, but with this promise of heat I propose we alter our schedule to go to town now instead of waiting until afternoon.

We walk together to the highway. Richard fishes in his pocket for the small change that will be needed for boarding. The sum is less than a nickel. A truck passes by us with a cargo of stacks of brooms. The straw for sweeping is not a natural fiber but colored plastic strands in the brightest possible tones of red, green, and blue. I love the color.

"I'm glad you think we should stay through the month, Richard." I know he's already subtracted three more weeks of park fees and the money necessary to get back to Tijuana. It's stored in a separate part of his wallet.

The bus lumbers to the curve. I realize I've developed an affection for it as it wheezes and jerks ahead. This machine has personality. There's no chance of a seat, and I grab for a pole to balance.

We stroll across the plaza and take a bench to finish a frozen Popsicle. Richard tosses the stick into a trash receptacle. Across from us are chairs propped on stands for the business of shining shoes.

"You really have stopped smoking. Now and then a little grass can't hurt."

For three days we have talked about everything but drugs. I've been well aware that Richard has been like a smoking factory of consumption. I haven't been able to stand around and watch after he brings out his pouch and papers, because I live on the edge of wanting it myself. I leave to look for shells, or visit the Shaws. I'll think of anything to do rather than watch the smoke that can tie the inside of my head into colored and curling bows. I'm sure he's even brought it up now because he would love to do a reefer.

"Never," I reply, feeling reluctant to unroll the topic to any more length.

"You know it's not exactly breaking the Ten Commandments."

I listen to him, remembering that when I met my husband he did have glass jars full of seeds to plant. Narcotics have always been a big part of his life.

"My reason is more subtle. I'm finished with drugs because they are just a crutch used to prop up my mood. My times of joy are going to be based on something real, not on what I've smoked."

"So Jesus is your new crutch," he charges.

"Oh, no," I laugh. "I need more help than that. Maybe God has to be my wheelchair."

I'm the first up to start toward the market. I know this issue is creating deep tremors in our relationship. We cross the street; Richard lags so I can't take his arm.

The meat market challenges our sense daily with its anatomy of animals. I want to buy onions and potatoes to fry with our fish tonight. We press by stands of waxlike candies to the aisles of produce.

> There's stalls of hot chilies,
> Fruits sun-dried to leather,
> All kinds of herbs
> For those under the weather.

We crowd in with women toting large nylon bags, mesh recipients for purchases from a myriad of heaped counters.

"Okay," says Richard. "I'll quit too."

I wheel around, not believing that what I've hoped for he's now said. I'm buying bananas and have to wait for the fruit and my change. The market is not the place to hug him and cry. Yet I know it's all in my face.

"I'm not going to hang around here, though."

Of course he can't make a stand to refuse grass and have it at less than an arm's length. We'll have to leave Mazatlán. It's too easy to get here. Every American that we've seen on the streets under age twenty-five has offered us a joint.

"How soon, Richard?"

"Let's get tickets now to start back to California tomorrow. We'll just get Noah and zip up the coast to Oregon. Rents there are still cheap, and we'll get jobs if we're going to hitch to Alaska at the first thaw."

Back at camp, with our departure tickets folded behind Richard's driver's license, we are in the final countdown before "death by bus." I dread the journey. Our camp seems full of charm. All living rooms would profit by a wall of lush foliage filled with twittering birds, besides the hi-fi of the sea.

"What should we do with this?" asks Richard, pulling out from the tent his bale of marijuana still wrapped in plastic.

"Throw it out into the Pacific," I suggest.

"No, I would rather bury it than do that."

The ground is still soft. It's all his act, and I don't want to interfere. He's really putting more under the ground than a sample of drugs. His will digs the hole, but his desire wraps it carefully and marks on a back page of my diary where it's buried.

Leaving Richard alone to do the rest of his work, I walk down to the water's edge. It's the first part of night, when only the closest planets and stars can be seen.

SAN DIEGO
February 11

We have crossed back into the United States. The border inspections were tolerable because we were innocent. The police hold no terror for those of good conscience. They checked everything other than our physical selves and samples of our urine.

I'm waiting for Richard outside a phone booth. He's calling his friend who has kept our dog. We want to get Noah and—we hope—sleep at their house before starting up the interstate highway to Oregon.

It's warm, and I'm feeling impatient because Richard is taking so long. I know I'm letting my exhaustion dominate me. But it has been about eight minutes, and those pay booth charges now exceed what we would ever spend for lunch.

In the midst of my murmuring Richard comes. He puts his arms around me and apologizes. He pulls me to him and strokes the hair back from a side of my face.

"Richard, it's fine that you talked that long." Love makes me sweet again.

"I've just made a decision, Laurel, that's going to hurt, but I think it's best." He's looking me in the eyes.

"My friend, Rick, he has a boy, and they all love Noah, so I said they could keep him. The dog is really happy. He doesn't need to be pulled up and down more freeways."

I know Richard's right, but I cry anyway. I love that old puppy. At least my sorrow has his comfort. Some women passing by stare at us, but I don't care.

"Let's just get out of LA." Even though we are south of San Diego, we have hours of overlapping cities to cross before real country. The idea of land here is an undeveloped lot.

We purchase staples. I could buy ten loaves of bimbo bread in Mexico for the purchase price of one here. We get peanut butter, apples, and milk.

I just don't want to see a dog, or I feel I'll cry again. We choose our place at the entrance ramp, and both of us raise our thumbs. We have an illusion that the harder we work our hands in solicitation, the sooner we'll get a ride.

A white station wagon slows down, and a woman in the passenger seat beckons for us to hurry. There's a teenage boy at the wheel, and two girls in the back move over to accommodate us.

"We're going north of Santa Monica."

Hearing we have three hours of guaranteed passage Richard helps me remove my pack and hoists it into the back along with his own. The girls sitting next to me are playing with plastic horses on their laps. There are rubber-band bridles and bits of scrap cloth girded around some of their toys. The oldest girl explains, with a forward nod, that her brother just got his driving permit.

It seems curious to me that they're giving us a lift. Women with children always pass us by. The lady in front explains that she occasionally helps people because she used to hitch once herself.

I fall asleep thinking there's a chain and I'm a link that in time will give rides too—only I hope my passengers will climb in white with snow or dusty from Alaska's back roads of summer.

PORTLAND, OREGON

February 18

Coming into Portland I compare us to geese that extend their feet to land in a familiar pond. We had a ride to Seattle but have jumped off by the road to Triple's house. Glancing down at my wedding ring I can see it shows signs of wear since it came from Triple's worktable.

It hasn't been even four months since our wedding, and I marvel at how far beyond that short shelf of time our experiences seem to extend. I'm ready for the quiet routines that can make a week seem like a long day.

Looking ahead I can see a woman in a long skirt digging in Triple's yard. I watch her for an entire block thrust her shovel into the earth and turn over the ground. She rests on her handle as we approach, the dark underside of the earth trailing out behind her feet like a peculiar shadow. I see she has patched holes in her clothes by stitching on pieces of an American flag.

"We're looking for Triple."

Seeing no response at the mention of his common name, Richard adds that he is also known as Ludwig Caminita III.

"Oh, he moved ages ago. He had a chance to buy some old place in the country, and we've rented this home."

Since we don't move, she adds that they have just finished getting rid of the stuff that he had left outside, and now intend to prepare the yard to be a garden.

"We would rather have fresh tomatoes than a lawn. I figure I'll put herbs here by the sidewalk where people are tempted to steal and plant the real vegetables up by the porch and in the back."

We turn now to seek Jack and Karen. Wistfully I examine every house we pass, wishing that somehow I had a place we could move in. Part of an old song lyric keeps repeating itself along the blocks toward their apartment:

> All I want is a room somewhere,
> Far away from the cold night air,
> And one enormous chair.
> Oh, wouldn't it be loverly!

We scan the room number board, but the Peterson-Anderson name has been replaced by an Italian surname.

"They must have moved," states Richard in a flat "these are the facts" voice.

With all my anticipation wiped away, I feel I have no strength left. Without the money for even the cheapest rental we have no option but to try to live and work out of our tent. We go over to the park blocks where there are benches to sit and make new plans.

"No, Laurel, all the campgrounds are in the mountains, and the police around here would be right on us if we tried to make a house out of our tent. We have about eight dollars left. What do you think we should do?"

I watch the squirrels as he talks. I bet they have a cozy hollow trunk filled with a bed of nuts. Without the leaves I can trace the fine lines of branches and see numbers of bird's nests.

"There must be some place for us."

My mind scans the idea of finding a tree house, or collecting enormous boxes discarded by the dumpster at the back of appliance stores. There's no such thing as an abandoned railroad car where we could cut windows and put geraniums into planter boxes.

"Maybe Karen still works at Import Warehouse," suggests Richard. "Let's give that a try."

Walking next to each other, we're well aware of all the stares cast at us and our backpacks. We are one step up from transporting our goods in grocery carts or sitting in doorways with paper bags. I can graph the decline of our possessions. First, we rented a two-bedroom house, followed by the cabin on the back of our truck, to now, a tent that is against the zoning laws to set up. We are exactly like the Russian folk story of the simpleton who traded the family cow for a succession of livestock and ended with a bucket of holes as his final possession. My thoughts dig a channel for tears.

I can see Karen through the glass working a cash register. Shedding my pack for Richard to watch, I run in to greet her.

Seeing me, she still has to attend to the business of ringing up a decorative wax paper umbrella, yet I can tell she is bursting to talk.

"Laurel, it has happened to both me and Jack too. We have become Christians!"

Karen waves to another girl to come over and take her place for a mid-morning ten-minute break. I follow her upstairs to the employee room. I can still see some of the bubble-letter signs that I made last October hanging over merchandise displays.

"When? How?" I ask on the upper landing.

"I went to this church that a friend, Adrian, invited us to visit. You've got to see it yourself. Well, they asked any who want to know Jesus in a personal way to come forward. I didn't know what would happen, but I just felt such a yearning . . .

"We are changed. I have been living with my grandmother, and Jack is with his mom. We just don't even want to live together anymore until we get married."

All my throbbing layers of complaints dissolve as I listen to her narrative.

"Laurel, there are so many street people getting saved that we have needed a place for people to come. A lot of us just need more of a supportive environment than two services on Sunday and one on Wednesday night. So, we all put in a little money and have just rented an enormous house. There's room for married couples besides what will be men's and women's dorms. This is my last week of employment, so I can participate full time in what's happening."

I can hardly talk because I'm so overwhelmed by the changes within a month. I assure her we want to move in.

"I'll call Jack and see if he can borrow a car to take you over to our new place. We have left the key outside so anyone can bring their stuff. This weekend we'll both be moving in."

I'm leaning over the backseat listening as Richard makes Jack repeat his last statement.

"That's right, it has six bedrooms, and it's only sixty dollars a month."

Across the Willamette Bridge we listen to Jack extol a Pastor Raymond Peters and their church, Glad Tidings. It is all, he explains, walking distance from our new rental.

As he drives into Portland's Albina District I respectfully note that neither of my friends even thought to mention that their new rental and congregation are in a solidly black neighborhood. Jack stops the car and points across the street to a gray block stone mansion from the early 1900s. Set on a rise, it has a curving walkway to a front porch. It's unlike any other structure in the neighborhood. An industrial business surrounded by a chain link fence has moved in behind it, and there's an assortment of small wood-frame homes built close to the curb.

I'm the first to jump out as Jack fumbles with the key to lock the vehicle. From the porch step I can see the beveled glass of the living room windows. Once the door swings open hardwood floors are revealed. There's an enormous entrance vestibule flanked by decorative wood pillars. A formal dining room is directly off the living room. The kitchen is lined with doors to the dining room, a basement, the upstairs, the backyards, and to what was once a maid's room.

On the second floor Jack indicates that the two large rooms are going to be dorms, but we can pick our own quarters from the rest. It's a solemn feeling to walk in and say, "This will be ours." The walls of the room I choose are pale yellow, and we're directly across from a bathroom with a claw-footed tub.

"Saturday the rest of us will join you when we can borrow a truck for beds and miscellaneous furniture."

"How many people?" asks Richard.

We had gone downstairs where we could sit on the kitchen counters and talk.

"Adrian Simila is really the head," says Jack. "Then, there's his younger brother, Eric, and they are both in a Bible school. There's me, and Karen, so with you there will be six of us in the beginning."

Jack excuses himself as he has to return the car. We get our packs and climb the stairs together into our new home.

We don't have hangers, so I drape our shirts and pants across the closet bar. Our toothbrushes go on a glass shelf and fit into side brackets built into the medicine chest. I feel exactly like the new First Lady moving into the White House after a long campaign I feared, at times, we would never win.

February 24

The Simila brothers are both Scandinavian blondes. I'm introduced to Eric first while he's carrying a double mattress through the front door. Adrian, behind him, is about twenty and nods without pausing in some song that keeps repeating the word "glory." They continue up the stairs, where they are going to deposit the bed in our room.

There're boxes everywhere, and the number keeps multiplying as I walk among the rooms. Karen is in the kitchen putting some cleaning supplies that her grandmother gave her under the sink.

"You know," she says, looking up at me from her kneeling position, "we're going to have to do the cooking. From the beginning when we first planned a community, it was assumed that we would take our meals together as a family."

I can hear the weight of what's expected of us in her tone. Plans can be like a winged horse, but their execution plod along pulling carts.

"I'll get some money from Richard. Let's go find a store and purchase something for tonight."

It feels about the same temperature outside as in the house. Cloud cover blankets the sky, but without threat of rain. A lot of the houses have big overstuffed chairs on the front porch, among miscellaneous furniture pieces, but no one is outside sitting and watching the street.

The shops are small, and some of the display windows are painted as a means of advertisement much as merchants everywhere decorate their glass at Christmas. There's a fish market with bright blue waves etching the bottom. Above them are smiling creatures of the sea with gaudy red and pink scales. The music shop has two black silhouette figures dancing in a bent and limber pose.

The one grocery is called More for Less and I mutter to Karen, "I bet it's 'pay more for less.' " We buy day-old bread at five loaves for a dollar, margarine, and oatmeal for tomorrow's breakfast. I choose carrots with onions to fry tonight as a vegetable with rice.

There's enough food for each of us to have a sack. We choose a different street on the way home to learn more about our neighborhood. Several men in overcoats are sitting on a rapid transit bench, but when the bus comes they wave it on without even lifting up their heads.

There's one storefront church. It has several names that were never measured by a calligrapher to fit the glass. "ROCK OF AGES" is in giant letters; "Holiness," and "Pentecostal," begin to shrink until "Church of the Golden Trumpet" is squeezed on the last fifth of the pane.

"Do they shout at Glad Tidings?" I ask Karen. I'm stifling the impulse to also inquire whether the congregation has ever fallen down in acts of ecstasy.

Karen shakes her head no. She tells of a Wednesday night foot-washing service once that had basins and towels. "I washed the feet of this older woman, who insisted that I should do it with her nylons on."

We are both chuckling when a young black man, leaning against a building, asks for some money. He explains it is for food. Instead of looking at us, he gazes a little to the right of our heads avoiding our eyes.

"Come and eat with us," says Karen. "We live just down the street over there." Balancing her groceries in one arm she points past a red-brick cleaners.

His eyes move to her face as he says, "I'm Leon." He offers to carry both of our sacks and walks beside us choosing to be closest to the street.

When we get to our walkway, Jack is on the steps with Richard carrying in some plants.

"Will you go get Adrian?" Karen asks, then turns to Leon and explains that everything is in disorder.

The tall blonde boy isn't singing now. He welcomes our guest as if every particle of his energy is magnetized by Mr. Leon of Albina.

They sit on a couch together, and Adrian explains that God has a plan for Leon's life. Listening to him outline the simple steps of surrender, I'm lost in my own reveries until I see Leon clench his mouth almost to grimacing. His eyes have been squeezed shut, and he begins to cry.

He wants to pray but says he doesn't know what to say. Everyone in the room is hushed by the power and the drama. Adrian helps, and I think of the forceps that are used for some births.

For the briefest instant I think I've crossed into a sphere where the invisible is revealed. Spots on every wall are appearing that are bright essences of color. It's not a host of angels beginning to reveal swatches of their robes, but rainbows. The sun has come out momentarily and is being refracted through all the beveled glass.

"That's for you," says Adrian to Leon while hugging him.

It's Jack who laughs and slaps his leg. "We should call this place the House of Rainbows."

As it's being agreed, Karen and I pick up the grocery bags to take into the kitchen. Someone has put a small table in the middle of the room while we've been gone. Instead of scrubbing four carrots that would be the portion for me and my husband, I empty two full pounds into the sink.

At dinner Richard says, "We have to agree to some rules that we can all live with." His tone makes it sound like we are about to discuss the Mayflower Compact.

The word "rules" produces immediate diversion. Eric laughs at the fact that it's compulsory for him and his brother to wear ties at Portland Bible College. He explains that they have just bought a rack at the Goodwill where they were on sale at twenty for a dollar.

I bring back the original subject by proposing that we have rotations of different crews to clean up after dinner. Karen endorses my suggestion and adds that there need to be regular posted chores for all aspects of house maintenance.

I watch the animated faces make their proposals for communal ethics and activities. No alcohol, no drugs, or cigarettes are ever to be allowed. Adrian wants one of the bedrooms upstairs to be designated as a prayer room. He's requiring group attendance for an hour every morning and night. Someone interjects that there should be nights when we keep praying until dawn.

Only Leon and I are quiet listening to the zeal of the new laws.

There will be daily street witnessing teams of two that are to stop pedestrians and discuss eternity. The bible college materials will be retaught to us from notes that the brothers will keep in their classes. Participation again is mandatory.

With my fork I separate my leftover rice grains and use them to make simple geometric patterns at the side of my plate. I feel that my involvement with this new House of Rainbows compares to being handed a pearl. But the pearl is not clean like the samples strung on necklaces; clinging to its surface are grains of sand that could be abrasive and irritating. I wonder how Richard is going to handle this.

February 25

I don't even own a dress to wear to this new church. I wish for something other than these pants that have traveled the world. Transferring toast to a plate in the oven, I wait for the others to come and eat something before leaving for Glad Tidings.

No one has altered appearance for Sunday. Both of Jack's knees have a web of blue strings crossing them where his overalls have shredded. Karen's wearing her green leather miniskirt. Leon, who brought over his bedroll, has on the same clothes as yesterday. The brothers, like Richard, are wearing the Sears basement blue work shirt. Everyone looks like what they so recently were, transients and drug dealers, but the conversations are about old hymns.

With the exception of Leon, we look like the white blight walking through the church foyer. Everyone, as my grandmother would say, is "dressed to the nines" or "looking like a million dollars." There isn't a woman without a hat or gloves.

We are welcomed and introduced to others by voices that so softly slur words that I'm reminded of warm honey. No one is "Mr." or "Mrs."—those words are brittle and belong to the outside. Here is relationship. I meet Sister Wells, and Brother and Sister Brazil.

Richard and I sit together in the large sanctuary as the Rainbows community disperses among the pews. There are several other counterculture people that have come too. One bearded man a few rows ahead has on a Tyrolean hat with a ribbon hatband. A girl in a long dress stands to wave at Adrian.

A rich, humming noise comes from the back. Like everyone else we turn to see a full choir approaching in two lines down the center aisle. Their voices are warming up, already full instruments of music before there are words. The choir members step in procession. There's nothing as pronounced as dance, but there's the making of it in how the foot rocks ever so slightly and the maroon robes sway with each step. Warbling words, they file across the stage like great purple-breasted birds. Solo voices challenge the energy that holds glass together.

The pastor rises with hands still beating out the last notes of music. His speech sets a kind of banqueting table. We have heard, and now we shall taste.

"Don't think that soul food is neck bones and greens." Raymond Peters wags his finger. "What feeds you is God's word." The pastor raises a Bible above his head.

Neither Richard nor I talk. Yet some in the congregation do punctuate points in the message with phrases of agreement. "Tell it," says a man behind me. "That's right," says a voice across the room.

There is the same invitation that Karen told me about at the end of the service. A number of hippies go to the front. It looks like the conversion of a pirate ship's crew. The pastor thunders over their heads to the people, "Man looks at the outside, but God looks at the heart."

Richard and I slip out the side door when the meeting is over.

We elect to walk back to the house by ourselves. Living now with five other people, we have conversed with everyone but each other. Again we need to check vital signs.

MAN LOOKS AT THE OUTSIDE, BUT GOD LOOKS AT THE HEART.

"What do you think, Richard? A week ago we were alone, and now we're part of a cast of thousands." I've only asked him his opinion about details at House of Rainbows, never the whole.

"I see it exactly like boot camp. Maybe this is our basic training until spring, and then we'll march to Alaska. Who knows? Maybe I'll start a church up there."

My breath catches for a moment with his announcement. I'm surprised at how my husband puts his all on whatever gust of wind is blowing. I'm glad it's religion and the North.

March 12

I pass by the big dining room table that's been set for breakfast. The food is late, and some of the brothers are already congregating. Their movements and glances at the kitchen door are like the impatience of drivers at intersections when a car ahead has stalled. They have no horns but to murmur. One boy has a watch that's now the object of consultation.

"Thirty minutes behind."

His complaint is directed at me. I mumble back that I'll check on things.

Two of the newer girls have the breakfast assignment. The shorter one is pouring pancake batter into the skillet. The reason for the delay is evident. She's cooking one at a time in the center of the pan.

"Look Marcie," I suggest, "pretend that you and Adele are creating a universe. Pour out some orbiting moons and a few small planets."

Shaking back her long, curly hair, Marcie relates that she's seen the week's menu that's posted on the side of the refrigerator. She thinks a couple of the food items are offensive and should have different names.

"It's just not a good standard, Laurel, to write 'deviled eggs,' and down here you have 'devil's food' cake."

I want to laugh, except her expression is too intense for humor. It's as if she's unmasked an insidious plot of demons to possess our national adjectives. No logic of mine will reach her, and I suggest she calls them what she wants.

Climbing up the back stairs, I take them two at a time. There's a window, and someone decorating has spelled out WELCOME on the sill. The medium for the message is seven blocks that each have a letter stenciled on its side. No one's looking. Quickly I rearrange them to say, OWE CLEM.

It's noisy in the hall from the banter in both dorm rooms. A couple of people are still praying, but their intercession for America is raised up with shouts instead of whispers. No one here believes God is dead, but they do behave as if he's deaf. The bathroom door is closed as it usually is. We are almost to the point of making appointments to use the tub.

Richard's gone. He had an early appointment at the church with the pastor. They want to start a printing press to reproduce sermon booklets and flyers we can give to people on the street.

Grateful for my teaspoon of solitude, I stretch out across the bed. Facing the closet I can see our packs leaning against the back wall. The sight of them evokes a yearning to move on.

Richard, too, is restless. We can't even speak of it, or we'll be airborne. Instead our conversations are the facts of duty, which for now act as sandbags and tether. From downstairs comes the cry for breakfast. I spring up, leaving wrinkles across the spread.

Karen is in front of me on the stairs. "I hope Brother Carp doesn't show today," she whispers.

Mr. Carp is probably in his sixties. We don't even know where he comes from, or how he heard of us. He's never been to Glad Tidings, and denies membership in any other Portland congregation. Somehow he's regularly at our door soliciting people for street witnessing.

As a house we didn't want to imitate the custom that recites some memorized ditty for blessing the meal. So, everyone speaks simultaneously phrases of appreciation, followed by minutes of silence.

Cliff, a new boy seated next to Leon, interrupts the quiet time to spout passages from Isaiah. I'm annoyed. I've been suspecting that we have a problem: competition among the members to demonstrate who has become the most spiritual. I fear there's too much emphasis on wanting to be a factory of wonder-working powers rather than to demonstrate character.

Marcie brings out the platter of pancakes. Cliff reaches out to grab for it, burrowing through the stack of hotcakes to those insulated and warm. The food is halfway around when we hear the sound of the front door opening, and Brother Carp strides into the room. Karen and I exchange looks. He never eats with us, but this time he walks up and down the room praying aloud.

"Who's at ease in Zion?" he cries.

"Maybe I would like to be," I mouth at Karen.

I have to go this morning with the team slotted for street evangelism. Karen is scheduled for the group going grocery shopping. Both Cliff and Marcie, with three others, run to get Bibles and coats.

Once the car doors have shut, Brother Carp bids us to pray without ceasing. It sounds immediately like a peculiar stock market bidding, or like auctioneers rehearsing. I look out the window breathing a petition for safety. Last time Carp went the wrong direction on a one-way street. I actually prefer the hubbub to listening as Cliff tells us how calloused his knees are getting from the extent of his prayer life.

We park in a free department store lot and confirm our time to meet again. I elect to stay by myself rather than accompany Brother Carp, who says he wants to go preach repentance in front of a palm reader's shop.

We're all to look for street people. I see Marcie across the avenue pass a stack of tracts to her friend, Adele. Two weeks ago she was a prostitute, and now she's worried if it's an offense to have "deviled" eggs on the menu.

I wave, then turn to walk away from them. The House of Rainbows is really a kind of nursery. Out of every row of babies some will grow into positions of distinction, while a percentage will never reach maturity. But the nurse never knows and is to bundle them all alike.

Crossing the street I remember that Richard and I are also in swaddling clothes, and the Nurse is invisible.

March 25

A row of bushes in the front yard flanks the long gray porch. I have watched the leaves unfurl through the weeks, monitoring the signs of spring.

Adjusting my purse I turn toward Glad Tidings where I'm to meet Richard. The weather is warmer, a bird sings, and there's presently a moment of sun. I think of the vivid colors now spotting the living room walls of our house.

After mailing some letters I look for Richard in the church business office. There are plans on the bulletin board for opening one wall of the sanctuary, and even constructing a balcony. Services have been packed. First it was only a couple of folding chairs that were needed. Then lines of them were set up along the aisles. The multiplication of members has now made remodeling a necessity.

"I believe your husband is down the hall."

I can hear Pastor Raymond Peters's voice coming from a supply room near the Sunday school class wing. I'm so used to hearing his voice divide scriptures that to hear him discuss the moving of furniture sounds like a parable.

Hearing Richard reply, I slip in to be with them. Peters is wearing a plaid jacket and discussing where to put machines.

"We can do our own stationery," he says. "There's some already with the church name, but I've been wanting to copy some like this."

I crowd forward to see the sample he's just pulled out of a locked drawer. At first glance I think it's a joke. It looks like a tear sheet from the *Harvard Lampoon*. An oval cut photo shows a man holding a microphone. His other hand, frozen by the camera, is gesturing to emphasize some point. Underneath is the name of the man's ministry in bold type, and the phone number to book him for meetings.

"Maybe we could use a little bigger picture of me, only put it in the center, here at the top. We can do business cards too."

It seems so tacky and vain. "Why?" I ask.

"I'm getting lots of invitations, and the income is to be clearly separate from Glad Tidings. Raymond Peters Ministries," he enunciates.

It is true that the pastor has been absent on lots of Sundays, and he's come back with reports of being in Australia and attending large conferences. The local paper has also focused attention on Portland's dynamic, integrated congregation.

"We're on to something big. Even my board doesn't understand. We should do everything we can to eventually have television broadcasts. That's where the profit is."

I excuse myself—wanting to be alone—and wait outside. The sun is, again, appearing in between clouds. The light transforms the lawn into a neon garden.

I'm disturbed. I realize that religion can become like a garment that hides a growing deformity of wrong motives. Whenever a lucrative business becomes the goal, something under the tailored folds is becoming crippled. Who then can walk straight?

Richard comes out. He has a Bible in a leather case that Jack made for him one night.

"What did you think of that?" I ask.

"I don't know," he replies slowly. "Sometimes, Laurel, even smelling smoke makes me yearn for a joint. Money and power have a scent too that tests people. The struggle can't be judged; only actions will tell its outcome.

"I did confide to Pastor Peters that we'll be leaving soon. He was really disappointed. He said the church was going to pay my fees to a special trade school where I could learn everything about printing."

Richard sounds flattered. Turning to look at him, I fall out of step with his stride.

I'm careful not to let any emotions affect my tone of voice. It is a definite career opportunity, and he should have the right to consider it.

"Would you want to go, Richard?"

I think of myself as a printer's wife. We would be no different from others, who intended to build yachts and cross oceans, but whose sea became a small lot in a subdivision.

Shifting my gaze from my husband's face, I look up at the treetops. The new leaves are beginning to cloak the fine tracing of winter's branches.

I sigh. Maybe we're facing the fact of adulthood. With Richard, I have reached for our dream as though it's a gold ring on a carousel. Now, it could be completely out of our reach, just like the plans of so many who settle for what is near at hand.

"At least being a printer is an honest life, and balanced."

"Don't be crazy," he cries. "I'm ready to go now!"

As he says it, so am I. There's a part of me ready to store away the silverware and eat with my hands. I love adventure.

Our steps synchronize as he tells me that we have been able to save eighty dollars, even after putting in our share to support House of Rainbows.

Coming up the house steps, we find Adrian has the blackboard propped against the old couch. He hasn't removed the regulation school tie, but it is loosened so the graphic of a painted palomino lies across his breast pocket. He likes diagrams, probably because his teachers like diagrams.

Only one person is using a chair; the rest are sprawled across the rug. I wish we had crept in through the back door and up the kitchen stairs. Duty demands we take seats and look attentive. I wonder why I fret at this; both of us have learned a lot. All my life my restlessness has been both a friend and an enemy.

During the dispensing of knowledge one student is sucking on long strands of his hair, and another rotates a finger in circles. No one is really still. One boy is maneuvering his tongue to push out his cheeks and lips. I'm no better. Inside my boots I'm curling and uncurling my toes.

What Adrian is saying is interesting, but it's competing with my realization that our waiting for departure has come to an end.

The house members, with us, have been woven together. Personalities have made the texture. Now, to say good-bye will tie the simple knots. Walking away will clip the threads. I can only hope we are doing what's right.

April 7

I'm glad we're alone on the porch. Right now my melancholy is delicately balanced with anticipation. Richard is ahead of me on the stairs, but turns for his own last look.

Lace tablecloths hang at the sides of the front windows imitating old-fashioned curtains. There was an impulse among some of the residents to make the front porch resemble a car bumper covered with stickers. Regularly, Karen and I peeled off statements of religious devotion. I left hanging above the mail box a shingle inscribed with a woodburning tool ARE YOU GOING TO HEAVEN? For all my yearnings to move on, the house looks dear to me as I turn away from it to follow my husband to the street.

Richard suggests that we should cross the street to solicit our ride. I can already tell my pack weighs too much. By this time it feels like a small chest of drawers strapped to my back.

In our place of high visibility my husband talks about the frozen lakes we are going to pass. He even estimates how wide their shoreline ring of thawed waters will be. He's only seeing tomorrow's country. I'm surprised that I'm not matching his pictures with my own eager descriptions.

GOOD·BYE

Instead, I'm remembering Karen this morning. She was finally wearing the corduroy pants that she had been embroidering
along the bottom band all month. She explained that her plan
was to stitch a psalm, "His Word is a lamp unto my feet," but
gave up after only completing "His Word is." I miss her, and Sister Wells, who last Sunday referred to my bandanna. She put her
arms around me in the church vestibule and said, "Girl, when
are you going to quit wearing that old rag?"

The sound of brakes brings us back from our separate reveries.
Two teenage boys stop in a car painted such a glossy red that the
chassis looks layered with dime-store fingernail polish. There
are slightly bigger tires in the back than in the front. The car is
about to pounce ahead. Since they are going to Tillamook, Richard pulls out the map to check the route along the coast. I tend to
notice picnic lunches and Styrofoam coolers in cars when I'm
hungry and need refreshment. Then, I'll shamelessly bring up
the subject of how smart they are to have a food carrier with the
hope of being offered a snack. Still full from the toast at the
House of Rainbows, I don't notice the cooler until one of the
boys flips up the lid to pull out some beer.

"Never touch the stuff," says Richard as a bottle is dangled
back at us.

I stop watching the clover fields and pastures of livestock to
stare at the boys. They had waited to drink until out of both city

and suburb, but neither the driver nor his partner can sip. They gulp in a competitive frenzy. It looks like the first to stop swallowing or move the container from his lips will lose.

"If they have any more, we better get out," whispers Richard.

The bottles, once emptied, are dropped to their feet, and they make no move for further libations.

On the outskirts of Tillamook a series of signs painted with a smiling cheese advertises some café. One yard, full of hand-crafted bird cages, has several suspended from poles and others laid in narrow rows along the yard. Pointing them out to Richard, I suggest that the proprietor should sprinkle wild seed to draw flocks of birds as an inducement for sales.

In the first block of the city street the driver pulls out two more Budweisers.

"Drop us off here," orders Richard.

The driver, first to be finished in their peculiar battle of excess, opens his window and tosses out the glass cartridge to shatter near the curb.

"Let us out!" cries my husband, leaning over the front seat. Immediately there's the sound of a siren, and the revolving red light of a squad car is visible out the back. The boy directly in front of me whips out his wallet and begins to stuff it down the seat cushion.

To the drone of the police car I'm protesting our innocence like a whining lyric inside my mind. The patrolman marches to the window and waves his hand in a gesture to silence all our explanations. We are ordered to follow him to the station. The siren is turned back on while he takes the lead. It makes us a curiosity as great as one of the seven wonders of Tillamook. I keep my face like a sphinx riding with the pyramids.

We carry our packs in with us. They are our symbol and proof that we are independent travelers. We need to be as polite as British schoolboys in fear of the headmaster's cane.

"So, you're on your way to Alaska," barks our beefy-faced interrogator. His first ring of fat bulges above his shirt collar.

"Oh, yes, sir," I reply, "and if you'll excuse us . . ." I gesture to the door as if the northern state is right outside and shouldn't be kept waiting.

He hands us a typed form with questions. The pen is chained to the desk. It includes a query of our mother's maiden names, and a blank line for listing our current banking institutions. Sarcasm rises within me; I want to footnote my right toe print. Finally, after being left alone for a few minutes, we are dismissed with a mumble about city ordinances not approving of vagrancy or hitchhiking.

"That's right," says Richard, with a wave that's part salute.

We march infused with the energy of escaping. A squad car passes us three times. They are not discreet. Our progress out of town is being monitored. I feel black. I feel the Star of David on my pocket. I'm an Indian after the white man got the railroad laid to the West. Finally the yards are the size of country acres.

We have short-distance rides. Successive cars take us but a few miles in a kind of local traffic leapfrog. On our side of the highway are hills that look as though they have never been shaved for their timber. The distant sea boils around giant rocks along the surf line. We hear there are still elk in these mountains.

In Washington, there are immediately taverns, unlike Oregon, where alcohol can be purchased only in state-run greenfront stores. There are a number of billboards advertising hard liquor. I read the captions, knowing their dark art is to hook into weakness: "One taste, and you are ours for keeps." Under one pouring decanter it declares, "Like the kind you learned on."

Three army men drop us off in the Olympic National Park by beach trail 4. Once on the shore we stir up the embers of a fisherman's fire and unroll our sleeping bags in a bower of driftwood to watch the sun set. Richard opens the map while there's still enough light to trace the colored road lines.

"Look, we'll get to Port Angeles tomorrow, where we can catch the ferry to Vancouver Island. I think customs there will be more lenient than at the border gates on the main freeway."

Richard has the same old Washington map that we used on the back of the International truck. I'm amazed that we've gone farther in one day than in those weeks of hauling our own cabin.

"We'll have to take a second boat here to the Canadian mainland." Richard runs his finger along the dotted line that indicates ferry services.

As the glow dims from the beach fire, we can see a single revolving beacon from a distant lighthouse. I think how good it is to have a night where I don't have to hear Cliff compare himself to the apostle Paul, then later know by how he smells that he must have borrowed a cigarette from Leon.

Yet, I wonder what new people came to the house today. I have loved reading the book of lives at the House of Rainbows, and now I can't see the daily print.

April 15

"There's a chance, Laurel, we won't be able to get into Canada."

"What do you mean?" I turn from the rail of the ferry *Coho* to stare at Richard. We can see Vancouver Island. The mouth of the harbor is enlarging as we chug through the waters.

"I've known this for a long time, even back when we were pulling our cabin." Richard sighs and turns from me to lean on the rail. His black wool cap is pulled low on his forehead accentuating his prominent cheek bones. His lips are compressed into a thin line beneath the fringe of his mustache.

"Border laws," he says. "The Canadian government requires a minimum of two hundred dollars, and more if they know that we'll be going up through the Yukon."

I put my gloved hand on his. I knew he'd been unusually quiet yesterday when we rented the four-dollar hotel room in Port Angeles.

Crew members, along with other passengers, have come out on deck to watch the landing. There are sea gulls squawking above us; they want deposits of breakfast bread to be cast upon the waters. We are just one note now in a symphony of motion. Ropes are being uncoiled, and some people have started their cars, ready to drive onto shore.

I can now read the city of Victoria's customs signs on the buildings directly ahead. The Empress Hotel looms on the horizon along with a fringe of distant fir trees. Yet, Richard's words have covered my view with a glass sheet. It may be a case of me pressing my nose against it, but not getting in. Being wistful will only steam its surface with my wanting.

We choose to be in the middle of the walking pedestrians. The phrase "Line up" is gone; we are instructed to "Make a queue" for examination. Richard has his wallet in hand for showing our identification. I feel like a living coin in the air; heads is forward, and tails we'll have to turn back.

There are enlarged professional photos of the northern Rocky Mountains, a basket of fish, and the mounted police.

"Where were you born?"

We answer each for ourselves.

"Have a good time!"

It was an interview of seconds. I feel younger and weigh less.

In another building, which has pigeonholes full of colored literature, Richard gets the schedule for the ferry to the mainland. He explains that there's a bus we can catch to the other side of the island for our departure, and after arriving in Vancouver it will continue on to deposit us at the city terminal.

I've been reading a sheet advertising the formal teas in the hotel whose lawns I could see from the deck of the *Coho*. Secretly, I wish to go there for a morning hour of elegance. My hands are going to rapidly age in the making of a pioneer homestead, and I wish to hold my last bone china cup before they are calloused. I can taste cream instead of milk, and imagine using silver tongs to lift up the sugar cubes.

Richard backs me farther into the corner to explain that the cost of this excursion package is like our insurance policy. We are so close to the border and would have all the wrong answers if subjected to any further questions. We must travel some distance north by bus before we can hitch again.

"We have well over an hour before departure. Let's go up to that grand hotel."

Richard laughs at my whim. It's deeper in me than he would guess. Instead, I follow him to look at fishing boats, but glance back at the Empress. I wonder if there's a woman inside who wishes to come out as much as I want to go in. She's been sentenced to high heels and nylons all the days of her life, and just for one last time would like to wear jeans and hitchhike.

The bus seems to fly us across the island, revealing a square of garden in each backyard. At the dock several gates restrain lines of vehicles waiting to board the ferry. The boat's three floors make it look like some triple-layered nautical cake.

We climb to a promenade that surrounds glass viewing plates for those who choose to sit inside. We continue up, past snack bars, to a sun deck. Richard leads me to benches at the stern of the ship. I know we have two and a half hours to chug through islands that are spread across the water like migrating whales.

Richard stretches out and soon sleeps with his head resting on his outstretched arm. I don't want to retreat from the wind and the sight of water whipped to the surface by submerged propellers. Contrasting with all the shades and sense of blue, between sky and sea, are the islands. The lush fir trees are one dark hue of green. There's a sense too of my own life changing again. This year has held my courtship and conversion. Now, I'm about to begin real work; we will soon take wild acreage and subdue it. We can't help but stabilize in its challenge. Any reservations about leaving House of Rainbows are evaporating.

I slip away from my sleeping husband. He doesn't need a guard. I want to experience the view from every side. My dream is to see a dolphin; it would be so lucky to spot one—as if I had found the four-leaf clover of the seas. By contrast the gulls are as common as grass.

The top horn blows our approach to the Canadian mainland. Richard is sitting up with both packs waiting for me. We descend to the lowest deck with the crowds who seek their own vehicles.

After the pure face of nature the profile of Vancouver looks ravaged by congestion and pollution. We want the first bus that can take us some distance north. Richard is looking up at a board that spells out the afternoon departures. Directly across is a formal photograph of the Queen of England; wearing a strapless formal, she has a proper two full inches of brocade above any cleavage.

"Let's get tickets to Hope." Richard is holding a map so new its creases have not even begun to fray. "It looks here to be the size of a small town, and there will be enough light to still thumb."

The name evokes a modern pilgrim's progress.

We claim the front seat, greedy for a view. Richard has learned from studying the map that we'll be passing through the mountains. The motor, constant and monotonous, is lulling me with rocking vibration. It is warm here too, being pressed between Richard and the window glass. Drowsiness is like a veil that begins to descend on me right after the suburbs of Vancouver. I'm fighting the layers that darken my mind. I want to see the Canadian Rockies that are a snow-covered band directly ahead. Yet my exhaustion is like a gauze with now only the tiniest mesh for light.

I'm fresh for the backpack, having slept most of the journey. We retrieve our gear from the luggage compartment in the bowels of the bus. It's hard to believe that this is still the same day as our 5:00 A.M. rising back in the Port Angeles hotel. It seems like such a long time ago we tiptoed past the sleeping manager to catch the first boat. The peaks are still visible, but behind us now. I regret again missing the mountain crossing.

Two brothers and a sister, all in their teens, give us a ride. I look at the girl while sliding in next to her in the back. She has on a miniskirt and fishnet nylons. They are French Canadians and, having lived on a farm, see Hope as their largest accessible metropolis. To them we have come from the ends of the earth.

The driver tunes the radio to Simon and Garfunkle. His eyes search for Richard in the rearview mirror. "What is Hollywood like?"

There's something in the tone of the question that I might duplicate if I found someone from another planet to question. It's news to them that there's no school holiday in May for the Queen's birthday.

The landscape changes. Mountains and rivers turn to sagebrush plains fenced for cattle. It's past nine o'clock at night and still light when they drop us off.

A truck driver is our next carrier. Expanses of water inhabited by wild ducks reflect the evening's pastel light. We finally climb out at the town of Williams Lake, 250 miles north of Hope.

Finding a local park, we find also the sign that states it has no camping facilities. The ring of cement picnic tables looks strong enough to stand for thousands of years. It could become the mysterious Stonehenge of Canada. We are too exhausted to look further. We just pull out sleeping bags, not wanting to erect our tent like a flag.

April 16

My pen casing has cracked. Only the narrow cylinder of blue ink remains for recording in my diary. There's no traffic at all. Richard and I are at the roadside in the wilderness. I'm bent at my work; my husband sees the green tank contraption first. Looking up, I exclaim aloud too. The visual sensation of the approaching machine must be like the wonder tiny children fee when exposed to their first parade float. We are amazed by its length and height.

The driver stops for us, turning off the motor so he can lower an aluminum ladder over the side. My questions after I climb aboard are in the same tone the boy last night used about Hollywood.

"This is an amphibian. It's constructed to be able to go down rivers as well as off roads."

Our host has a grizzled chin and is wearing an old baseball cap. He's not a man who lives with mirrors. Looking away from the driver, I see our vehicle is full of aluminum cases and large drums.

"I just pick a place to go in the water, and with my equipment I can pump the bottom for gold."

He volunteers to drop us off at the next town. Even the slowest cars whiz by. We proceed at the speed of a tractor.

"With luck you'll get a lift straight on to Dawson Creek. It's only about 150 more miles." Our driver uses his hand to motion to the highway ahead. The gesture means something, since his vehicle can drive in any direction.

"That's where the Alaska Highway officially starts," adds Richard.

"You'll find that Milepost 0, kids, in the middle of the town."

While our driver is speaking I see the first frozen lake. The swell of land and timber has kept its surface in shadow from the sun. Richard exclaims over a log barn built behind a cabin that is also chinked with clay. That, with the posted name, Moose County, is all the evidence I need that we have crossed into real country.

"A guide lives there who leads hunting expeditions. It's a shame that it's becoming so built up in these parts that shooting deer from your back window is just a memory."

The town that we descend into from the ladder's eight rungs is only on one side of the road. A single pump dispenses gas. There's a tiny store where every canned good is seventy-five cents more than in Hope. Along the far wall is a three-table café where a couple of men sit drinking coffee. I can see from the posted menu that an order of toast is more than I would pay for two loaves of bread.

Buying nothing, we go outside and strip off our packs where the parking lot asphalt flows back into the road. There's no reason to even raise our thumbs.

"I wish everyone at House of Rainbows could see how far we've come in four days."

One of the coffee drinkers comes out the door and motions to us while striding to a pickup truck. "Dawson Creek," he sings forth, much like a tour leader gathering his passengers.

"Just want to warn you," he says, once we're up in his cab, "I believe in going fast!"

Richard turns to make sure our packs in the bed behind us are secure for high speeds. After the amphibian, which was so slow I could check the patterns on roadside rocks, we're now flying. There are some more cabins, like little blinks of brown logs, in the stream of pines out my window.

A number of large granaries line the road. We are dropped off by the "0 mile" marker topped with three flags for Canada, the States, and the Yukon. Every shop sells the post's image on picture postcards, along with glossy photos of moose.

Richard picks the Mile 0 Hotel to inquire about rates. We need to clean through our packs and discard every extra thing contributing to the weight load.

The proprietor believes a sign should cover every function. Besides the room cost, five dollars, there are printed statements against credit and loud noise. The back wall is filled with simple, misspelled notices. The management is not responsible for any left valuables, and only one bath is allowed per guest, per night. "The tub," it says, "is at the end of the hall upstairs."

After paying, we walk down a narrow corridor to find our number. The first notice in the passage states, "There's no ice machine on the premises."

Our room has a double bed and a chair. Hooks have been drilled into the wall to compensate for the fact there's neither a closet nor a chest of drawers.

I expected signs for room government, like "Don't wear your shoes to bed," or "Put cigarettes in ashtrays," but the walls are bare.

ALASKA HIGHWAY
April 17

We are both filthy. The paved road ended in the first town after Dawson Creek. It's already evening, but it looks like late afternoon. Every ride that passed us by also covered us in a great plume of dust. I can see it on my skin. My hair feels coarse, and my clothes have lost some of their color in this fresh film of dirt.

"Where should we camp?" Richard asks.

I laugh in reply. There are hundreds of square miles radiating from every compass point. We could put a tent anywhere. Having seen two wild moose after Fort St. John, I'm only wary of choosing clumps of grass. I don't want to think about being trampled or gored.

Richard points to a natural glen in a grove of poplar trees and bushes. After knocking a mosquito away from my eyebrow, I follow my husband up the slight incline. While waiting for rides, there have always been tiny buzzing insects, which prompted me earlier to break off a branch and wave it over my head.

"Did you hear what that one driver said about Yukon law?"

The question needs no answer; we were together when it was explained that the Royal Mounties consider it a misdemeanor to pass someone on the highway who motions for a lift.

"So, Richard, every tourist flies right by, but the local people are stopping."

Richard pulls out the tent, which we unfold and secure with stakes. I'm thinking about one woman I met today who was in overalls putting in her own transmission. Our driver pulled up to her cabin in the gesture of a neighbor to ask about things. She wiped the grease on her pants and invited us in for coffee, but our host declined.

"What a gal," he had said to me once back on the gravel highway. "Homesteading women know how to be completely self-sufficient."

Richard is pulling out his green mummy bag.

"Don't expect to be kissed tonight, as there's too much danger of creating mud."

I crawl in the tent behind him dragging my sleeping roll. A number of mosquitoes have come in with us through the open door. Unfortunately, there's no netting on the windows, making it impossible to kill every insect.

"What was that lady's name that we met for a few minutes?" asks Richard.

"Helen, and I've been thinking of her too."

It's bad enough that the mosquitoes want to draw blood, but the fact that they buzz continuously makes them intolerable. Somehow, a few have crawled inside my sleeping bag, but most seem to be swarming by my ears and sizing up my cheeks for a landing. I'm getting hot and more uncomfortable with my twisting and waving in defense.

"Imagine," says Richard, "she butchers and wraps game besides being a mechanic."

There's definite awe in his voice. I can't even hand him the right tool, and I've moaned about blood in grocery meat packages. The driver said she was a typical homesteader and had lived alone on that claim for a number of years.

Sitting up to kill bugs, I can see them actually sifting through the window like a fine vapor. There are itching welts along my forehead and arms. I hate insects that whine and pierce my skin!

Richard tells me to settle down. I'm turning into a windmill beside him with my thrashing.

"You know, Laurel, you're going to learn how to do all that too. Once we get a truck, I can show you about maintenance. In no time I bet you'll be hunting and trapping too."

I know that if I were to remain on this planet another five hundred years, I couldn't learn to do that stuff. I'm starting to sweat profusely as I have to secure the drawstrings tight around my neck to protect myself against these insects.

"Aren't these bugs bothering you?" My voice is frantic and shrill.

"Not particularly," says Richard. "I don't bother them, so they leave me alone."

It's such an untrue thing for him to say that I instantly feel hostile toward Richard—and Helen too, who can quarter dead moose. She's a sculptress of a haunch, and hating her, I start to cry. My face is dirty and sweaty. My bug bites itch, and I'm rubbing my eyes with a vigor that I'm sure will make me lose my lashes. I'm envying a woman that I met for four minutes, and I wish I were in the Empress Hotel for more than tea. I want a real room with a bath.

"Good grief," says Richard. "What's your problem?"

"I'm being tortured by mosquitoes!"

Life and death in a relationship depend on attitudes. Richard is kind. I'm so glad for the change in his voice. I remember reading, too, that the divorce rate is higher in Alaska than in any other state.

I don't think anything will stop the incessant whining, but I can keep the bugs from marching across my face like Sherman to the sea, biting everything. There's an extra bra in my pack with a lacy cup. I insert it in my sleeping bag as a breathing hole. If I can just relax, I want to lose my consciousness of every discomfort.

Maybe I'll never be fluent in speaking all the languages of a homesteader. But maybe I can learn the syllables, and one is courage. I can see the insects walking and probing not more than one inch from my eyes.

April 18

"I tell you, Richard, the mosquitoes were still there in the morning. I did see about twenty of them hanging upside down in the top folds of the tent. They were waiting for my arms to come out."

We are walking along the serpentine highway hoping to come upon a mileage marker. We want to know the distance we've traveled from Dawson Creek. Some of the lakes look blind with ice. There is a lot of snow on the mountains, and if we should dig, there's a permanent stratum of frost. Yet, even clad in our coats, we know it is spring.

We can see the dust first. It is billowing up, dissipating into the air behind a Volkswagen van. If it passes us, we'll instinctively turn from the road blind in its wake and hold our breath. It's in range now, showing a Yukon Territory license plate. Besides numbers, it shows a miner bending over a gold pan.

The car does brake. We thrust back the sliding door for me to climb in with our gear while Richard takes the single seat in the front.

Our driver has on a blue Hawaiian shirt and a polka dot cap.

"I'm Ogertschnick." He speaks with an accent reminiscent of European cafés. He's a bush welder going to Whitehorse, the capital of the territory.

"There's going to be a bingo game tonight, but unless the stakes are high, I won't play. Gambling is about the biggest entertainment we've got out in our camps. Once, I even won $9,500 in a blackjack game."

I lie back against my pack still tired from the emotions, and conditions, of the night. I'm slouched enough to see a band of sky above the trees. Eagles and smaller hawks glide without effort.

The sidewalk in Whitehorse is simple plank boards. Among some rustic cabins and shops are a number of bars, including the Malamute Saloon.

"You'll find Indians starting to line up even before the doors open," says Ogertshnick. "They get treaty money each month from the government."

I want to get out and see an exhibit of native art curios in a window.

Three log cabins are built on top of each other, which our host explains was the first hotel back in the gold rush. The one movie theater is playing Hitchcock's *North by Northwest*. I exclaim over a couple of men walking with guns strapped to their hips.

"You'll get used to all this since you are going to make a claim in Alaska. I tell you, when I first came here from Austria I was camping by a stream and terrified by the giant rats coming out of the riverbank. It was Indians who told me they were only beavers."

Once out on the street I feel compelled to get clean even if I have to lie naked in my sleeping bag in the corner of a Laundromat while every bit of clothing is washed and dried.

"Come on, Richard, let's go and get a hotel room."

"Why, we don't need that! We can camp anywhere! There're no restrictions like in the States. Let's just hike out a little way and put up our tent."

His speech makes me feel like crying again. I can't bear the idea of another night like the last one. I walk briskly ahead of my husband to try and gain some self-control. Every argument for getting accommodation is bristling. All the words surfacing within me have teeth, and my impulse is to snarl at him. Dirty, tired mad dogs foam easily at the mouth.

"Laurel," Richard takes my arm. "You'll only get covered with dust again tomorrow. We've still got over eight hundred miles more of gravel before the border."

"Needs are not always practical," I retort.

Richard is also angry. "Look," he says, "we need to save everything that's left for getting our start in Alaska. Those boat and bus tickets took a real chunk of our money."

Out of the corner of my eye I see a couple of Haight-Ashbury hippies stroll by. It's the beadwork on their sleeves that I first notice. The two men each have their hair pulled back into a long braid. They look like rich drug dealers on vacation.

Maybe they are staying in a facility where we could put our bags on the floor tonight and at least sleep inside away from mosquitoes. I run ahead, crying out, "Hey, you guys, please stop a minute."

They swivel and stare. These are not city boys on an adventure, but full-blooded Indians wearing ceremonial clothes. Their eyes are piercing as I back away apologizing.

Richard has caught up with me. "What is wrong with you?" His voice has all the tone of a parent correcting a child.

Men with guns pass on either side of us. Everything feels violent and primitive.

"Now, there you two are." Ogertschnick pulls up to the curb

in his Volkswagen. "I went to get myself a motel, and the only unit left has two bedrooms. Why don't you share it with me?"

My appreciation takes form as the song of the slave. "Swinging low, sweet chariot, you have come to carry me home."

Ogertschnick points to the door of what will be our bedroom and to the bath down the hall. He has rented a full suite with a small kitchen and central sitting room.

I begin to pull dirty clothes out of my pack that I can scrub by hand. While kicking the garments into a pile, I can hear through the wall that the shower is being adjusted. Deep in the sound of the water is music. I can imagine a full miniature symphony now playing in the shower head.

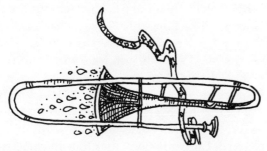

Richard has unfolded the map across the bed. His finger traces the line of the Alaska Highway to estimate our remaining miles according to the corner scale. "With real luck, Laurel, we could cross the state border in three days."

That wouldn't be luck at all, but I think of an older word used by generations before ours.

"Richard, that would have to be 'Godspeed.' "

ALASKA HIGHWAY
April 22

I watch the trailer attached to the hitch of the pickup truck. We have been riding in the truck bed for two days with our legs stretched out under tarps. I can't see the words from this angle but know they are stenciled on each side of the motor home. Named after the couple who picked us up yesterday, the trailer is called the Potter's Ideal Potty.

This vibrating brown-and-white tin box distracts from my vision of raw river beds, forest, and craggy mountains.

"We must be almost there," says Richard. We both yearn for the border as if our year has been like a game of Chutes and Ladders or Candy Land's molasses trap. Finally we'll be home; it's just a matter of rolling the right numbers. We both look for the mileage post.

We reach the Canadian border station and find an officer in uniform. I can hear Mr. Potter's voice complain of the dirt deposited in their trailer from the past thirteen hundred miles of gravel. His wife echoes him with, "Mercy, that dust!"

Obviously the border guard has heard it before. He has his fast, polite answer. "We are just free with our real estate, Ma'am."

Richard nudges me and points at the Alaska state flag. The sound of gravel that has been such an integral part of this journey is gone. We are on quiet black asphalt.

The outskirts of Fairbanks don't look like much. Almost every business is constructed along this main road, and behind it is a wave of simple houses with tiny yards. It's like going back in time to see the building of America along the highway and railroad lines.

We're eager to get out. Already we have rolled back the tarp and moved our packs to where it will be easy to lift them off. The Potters pull to the roadside. We know their plans are to find the local trailer park that they showed us in their guidebook.

We walk toward the center of Fairbanks, which is an area only about four blocks long by three blocks wide. My first impression is that Fairbanks is just impersonating a city. I want to buy mosquito netting and imagine there's such a demand it would be featured in glass show cases toward the front. Richard has been recommending that we purchase a cheap canteen. Often we were thirsty in the pickup but could do nothing but stare at lakes and wish the rig would stop. I want postcards too. What I can write and mail is my only thread of connection with House of Rainbows. Last, we will buy the staple loaf of bread.

One side of Fairbanks is bordered by a river. After our last purchase, we walk to its bank. Here alone do I find a marker that acknowledges the position of this northern spot relative to the cities of the world. We are about eight thousand miles from Bombay, and the farthest point marked is Capetown, thirteen thousand miles away.

I look out at the silvery movement of the river. The sign has turned the earth beneath my feet into a globe. Somewhere inside of me I can feel the love of adventure stir like a creature that nests within.

An older man is seated near us on a bench rolling a cigarette. Stripping off my pack I put it at the far end from where he is sitting.

"Breakup is earlier this year."

I have no idea what he means and turn from balancing my knapsack to look at him.

"Breakup?" I ask. This isn't the type of person who offers comment on how the deprivations of Alaska affect relationships.

"Oh, you know, that's when the ice on the Chena River here melts enough so it can begin to flow."

He stops talking to rub his chin and transfer his cigarette to his left hand.

"Everyone makes a bet on the day, and it becomes a rich little kitty for the best guesser. Different every year too. I see you're tourists."

"We're here to make a land claim," says Richard.

"I wouldn't bother with these Yukon flats. Go over toward Anchorage. You can buy maps there at the Bureau of Land Management, then go stake the piece you want first. After you register it, then you've got to build something you can live in."

He stops speaking to suck on his cigarette. His words have the effect on us that a bow has on an arrow. Thanking him, we turn and set out on that course.

Walking back along the main street, I notice that the old man, like every other resident, referred to winter. There's an exterior thermometer on most of these buildings, now registering fifty-two degrees. The clouds on the horizon look rounded into snow mounds. To us, the phrase "forty degrees below" is just a string of simple words—and an experience awaiting us.

"Laurel, I haven't really counted the change in my pocket, but our money is low enough that we'll have to find some kind of work in Anchorage. That city is about four times bigger than this one, so we should have some opportunities."

We've both been meditating on realities. Side by side we are considering cash and ice. Starting to hitch I yearn to sleep rather than solicit rides. Again, I wish for a watch. The sunlight is like a makeup that covers the real age of the day.

We are out of the Canadian jurisdiction that requires resident motorists to stop. After a stream of cars passes us, we get a short lift along the turnoff to Anchorage.

Mount McKinley, captive in ice since before history, broods in the distance. A sign declares that we've entered the refuge area for bighorn sheep. We walk, and there's no sign of house or human. Nature here is naked and at full stature. It can evoke in me a passion for the land. More than the beauty, it's the sense of freedom. There's plenty of acreage with inspiring views back in the lower states, but with it come building inspectors and permits and fees. I have come home, and I'll think of the mosquitoes as my watchdogs that scare away strangers.

Richard is pretending to be a fat frog that lives on bugs. He's making it into a ditty of doggerel and unrolls his tongue as if to dine for the chorus.

After days of shrinking back into gullies to avoid the dust when a car passed us, I tense as if ready for flight now as soon as I see the approaching station wagon. A middle-aged woman stops for us. The backseat of her car has been collapsed to accommodate cases of canned food and paper plates and cups.

"There's still some room for you, I'm sure." The bench seat next to her is empty. I let Richard fit our packs between a Hormel chili box and a 18-can carton of Campbell's soup.

Sliding to the middle, I glance at our driver, whose polyester sweater and pants are stretched over hills of fat.

"Run me a little restaurant up by some mining claims; it's on the other side of this parcel of state-owned land."

"Short winter this year," she comments. "We didn't get our first real snow until the very end of September."

"What do people do?" I'm becoming increasingly curious about the occupations of people held in small rooms for six months when it's dark outside.

"It's different with everyone," she murmurs. "Some couples sure fight a lot."

Something about her chuckle implies she has been in a few arguments herself.

"Really, it's different with everyone. A lot of us can't wait for spring, but we love winter best. A friend of mine, a taxidermist, just stuffs some of the animals from his trap line while it snows outside. I like to cook, myself, and eat, and read. Some folks keep dogs and do a lot of sledding with their teams."

Hilma asks where we are going and suggests we stay in one of the state-maintained emergency winter shelters for tonight.

"Look at that!" she cries. "Damn nuisance, should shoot em all!"

"What?" We ask in unison. We can see nothing through the trees but a lake and an occasional grayling breaking the surface where it has thawed.

"Beaver dam," she explains with her lips twisting out the words. "They mow the trees down until the bank erodes, and that can flood this road with the spring runoff."

Hilma points out the last curve before the shelter. Pulling to the side, she offers us a couple of cans of food.

"There should be a pan, and wood for the stove. Most likely anyone going this way is bound for Anchorage. You'll be there easily tomorrow."

It's a mystery how the bugs are waiting for us. I'm not even out of the car, and I hear one whine by my ear.

Once we are inside it's a little like playing house. The beds are the same government-issue that new soldiers use and that illegal aliens use in detention centers. I look around and wonder what Richard and I would do in here for six months. What we'll be able to construct this summer will be less than a third the size of this room.

Rolling out my sleeping bag on the bottom bunk I think how much I would love to sew a quilt. I can even imagine squares embroidered in purple, turquoise, and rose that could cover me the next winter as I recline, maybe with twins.

Once in bed, I shorten my prayer to consider names for infants. Sorting through the proper nouns of old classmates and characters in books, I settle on Matthew and Hannah.

April 23

Our driver grunts that he will drop us off in Anchorage. His silence makes silence. This morning the clouds are a net across the sky. My attention is on the grandeur of the mountains, but I'm noticing a tightening of the overcast mesh to allow a little blue to be visible. The darkest area is directly ahead. As in all things, I never appreciated how wonderful the weather has been until seeing this threat of a storm. If the temperature should drop, we could even be engulfed in snow.

I glance at our driver. He is not an old man, and I look for a ring to see if he has a wife. There is a wedding band, which makes me wonder how anyone could live with a spouse so ramrod still. His manner is that of a guard on permanent duty at Buckingham Palace. I'm glad for Richard, who can pretend to eat flies.

With the sighting of the city skyline comes the rain. There are no introductory drops on the windshield, but instead a deluge. Only directly behind the stroke of the wipers is there any visibility. I can see some cars have pulled to the side for safety, but our driver only slightly decreases his speed. Without comment he squints his eyes to see through the curtain of water. I hope we have enough money for a hotel, but I'll wait until I can ask Richard alone on the sidewalk.

"You know, Laurel, we don't have it."

We are standing under the awning of a sporting goods store, having got out at the first intersection where our driver could stop for us.

Looking over Richard's shoulder I can see a display of tents that have been set up on a platform at the level of the window glass. The advertising placard states they are designed to withstand Arctic cold. I can't help but wistfully compare our little triangle of canvas to these aerodynamic designs.

"What do you want to do?" I ask. While speaking I'm also checking to see if it's getting cold enough to make a subtle cloud vapor at my lips, but no ghost of winter past forms by my mouth.

"Let's go find some café, Laurel, where I can get coffee and we can figure out a plan."

Before moving from the one protected spot of pavement, we pull out our rain ponchos and draw up the hoods. Richard points to a bakery down on the other side of the street. As we open the door the smell of the fresh bread reduces me to want.

Holding our hot rolls in napkins I choose the table away from the door.

"We have seven dollars left, now that we have just spent this change," says my husband as soon as he's taken one sip from his cup.

"Look, Richard, as soon as this storm clears I can start asking for work at restaurants."

With this pack under my poncho I would resemble some inflatable rubber toy making an application. No one hires a waitress who's green and looks as though she can bob around in bathtubs.

"The trouble is, the weather could stay this way for days," is his grim summary.

While savoring the last bites of my bread I wonder where we can sleep. I dread thumbing to the outskirts of Anchorage and putting up a tent in the pouring rain. Yet, we have no alternatives. An emergency winter shelter is too far into the country to make work accessible. Depression feels like a magnetic force field sucking away all sense of adventure. We are homeless. I wonder how long we can sit here before the bakery clerk begins to stare. I can feel the stirrings of despair.

Richard is looking out the window. Even though the storm has not abated, neither is it getting worse. Because of the hurricane in Mexico, I realize I'm expecting a like experience, only with a northern cast. If we find a campground, there will probably be avalanche warnings.

"Let's go," says Richard. I follow him feeling I'm in a dark sphere that broods and murmurs. At least only my feet are getting wet, and the multitude of bugs have found shelter away from me.

I point to a church with a suggestion that maybe we could sleep in a classroom. Richard nods in mute agreement, then reaches to test whether the door is open.

Seeing the sign indicating the church office, I feel like part of an equation in a divine ethics test. Are they going to give to those who ask of them?

A woman rises from her desk to greet us. She looks from our faces to our feet, checking whether we've tracked mud down the hall. Fumbling in her speech, she struggles for words to express what I discern is going to be a refusal to help.

"We are neither licensed nor insured for providing casual accommodations."

Feeling embarrassed, I wonder what book she goes by. I've introduced us as Christians. My dignity is fragile, and now I must turn from her and not have less of it.

"Wait," she cries. "Just a few blocks away the Salvation Army runs a relief shelter."

Richard repeats her instructions, and we are back outside in the storm. Drafts of wind blow the rain upon the asphalt. There's constant noise. My bowed head is recipient of a relentless tattoo.

The front window of the Anchorage mission has the same red neon that restaurants use to advertise, but here it says, "Jesus Saves." The vestibule is wet. There's been a lot of foot traffic from the street. The management is big on religious art. This is a regular gallery of scenes of Israel. Proceeding into a large meeting room, we see long benches facing a lectern.

A woman with snowy hair rises from a corner piano bench. Dressed in the peculiar uniform of her religious works, she states her name as Miss Esther Thornton. In clear, clipped tones she explains there are both a men's and a women's dorm, but no accommodations for married couples. Both dinner and breakfast are served, but tables are segregated, and again we can't sit together. We agree to these terms. Attendance is also "compulsory" for a meeting every night at 7:30.

Her precise words are affecting me like helium. I could float for relief at having guaranteed food and shelter.

"You will be allowed to remain here seven days. No one seems to be hiring now in the city, but we do get calls for casual labor, which are announced or posted.

"My assistant is out. So one of you will have to wait here while I guide you to the dorms. Oh," she says, "and above all else, no alcohol is ever allowed."

She is so fierce in this last declaration that I can almost see her attacking saloons with a hatchet. I resist the impulse to lift my right hand in a formal vow of abstinence.

Richard remains, and I follow Miss Esther up a set of stairs. I know by her age that she was raised with the phrase "Ladies first." Her gait is too fast for me to walk by her side. I watch her knot of hair riding exactly like a compact snowball at the nape of her neck.

The dorm isn't the expected corridor of beds, but a series of rooms with four metal cots, each in a corner. The women that I glimpse through the doorways appear to be mostly Indians or Eskimos. Seeing the facility's commander, they drop their voices and regard me with curious eyes. I must look to them like three hundred pounds wrapped in dripping plastic. With a gesture that points to a door, and a reminder that chapel will be soon, I'm sent to a room on the right.

Two women, sitting across from each other, stare at me. One has shocking yellow hair. Because of the exposed one-inch black roots she looks like a university experiment testing the rate of hair growth. The other roommate is also an Indian, but her hair hangs in traditional braids except for deep bangs that are cut and set in pin curls.

Giving first my name, I struggle out of my poncho then turn to learn of my companions. Twila and Annette are each from different government land grants north of Fairbanks. They came to the big city for work and have obviously fallen on difficult times. I would ask them everything, but their answers to my rudimentary questions are brief and terse. They are just filling in blanks where I yearn for paragraphs and replies that could fill a sheet. In addition they ask nothing of me, so I'm to return the same courtesy.

After stowing my pack next to a dresser, I unfold a stack of linen and make my bed. The wind outside sounds like its' being forced through the neck of a bottle. Yet, hearing it from inside a warm room muzzles the weather. It now feels domesticated, on a leash, where outside it was wild and threatening.

The wage for the night must be paid by attending the meeting. I file out with expectancy. Everyone emerging from other rooms takes a long time to look at me, but they say nothing. I can feel I'm an outsider; I'm of Irish descent and from the lower forty-eight states. I listen to every small exchange in the hall and on the stairs. There are references to a number of men who are also mission residents. The direction of their affections is analyzed, and physical form praised. I hear complaints about the food. Apparently a lot of game has been donated to the center, and moose meat is minced into every night's main dish.

I look for Richard as the men descend from a like staircase across the assembly room. Around me I sense some static as eyes seek eyes across the aisle, and there's a shuffling for seats closest to the assembling body of the opposite sex. A few bearded, long-haired boys are present on treks north, but mostly the residents are native Alaskans.

Sitting in the very front, I'm farthest from the aisle. Miss Esther has attired herself in a Salvation Army regulation bonnet. Like the headpiece on a nun's habit, it reflects an age before the automobile. One incongruous thing is the music on the piano before her. It must have been because they were so frayed that she taped the disintegrating sheets onto sturdy cereal box wrappers. So, the colors of Kellogg's corn flakes, and Post raisin bran enliven the rack above the keys.

The commander opens in music and pounds the chords. Her choice, a series of hymns written at the turn of the century, will not sway this room of children born in the wild.

Once upstairs Annette puts her bobby pins back on her curls, while Twila dabs the same shade of red over her already polished fingernails. I get in bed acutely missing the people that came with their needs to House of Rainbows.

I think about Miss Thornton's message on the nature of Jesus. But I yearn to re-dress the fact in today's words and discard the images of rustling silk bustles. I wish for a chance to speak.

A Trapper kept sled dogs, and one of his pups was lost. He went to seek it before the bear or timber wolf could devour it.

ANCHORAGE
April 28

I can hear musical instruments. It sounds like a band marching in place about three blocks away. I'm tired of looking for a job again today. It has been an exercise in hearing the variations of no. I've been asking for anything now, even kitchen cleanup and busing tables, but everywhere it is still the same refusal.

I decide to explore the reason for this bursting forth of John Philip Sousa, and cut across a parking lot. Richard is helping unload a truck for three hours at minimum wage. We are to meet at the Bureau of Land Management on Cordoba Street to study available areas and learn exactly how to mark our claim.

Coming around a corner I find a decorated grandstand with army officers addressing recruits, who stand at attention in lines of ten by ten. I feel I'm looking into a time warp. There has been no smoke of draft card burning here. Parents are photographing their sons in uniform, and the music is of honor and valor.

I continue to the Bureau of Land Management, where there's an etching of a buffalo above the double doors. I would have passed by a rendition of an eagle or an elk, but the fact that the creature of their logo is almost extinct seems significant. How long before the game here will be gone and the rivers polluted?

There are cases of green maps of the wilderness inside, like a library, only with volumes of land. It's overwhelming to consider that every point of a compass radiates into property we can claim. I've asked the Indians at the mission what to look for, and their advice was to pick a stand with tall birch and native grass because gardens do better there. We are to avoid blueberry bushes because they grow where there's no depth of soil over the permafrost that can ruin the foundation of a home.

Richard strides through the door and joins me, announcing we have another nine dollars but there are no work opportunities for tomorrow.

I've been staring into an enlarged map of the state that is divided into numbered sections. Less than one percent of the available land has been surveyed. Now, we are to choose the area for our plot and then go over to the Geological Survey office to purchase our specific maps.

Feeling paralyzed by the range of choices, I want to shut my eyes and dab in the wilds of chance.

"We'll need highway access," says Richard, which narrows our concentration to the property that borders the few red lines of road.

We need advice. Time and money could be lost traveling to some uninhabitable piece of terrain, forcing us to return and repeat this very process.

When lost, I look for gas stations for counsel. I've always bothered librarians and gone to information booths at shopping centers. Looking over at the employees in a separate area of desks, I see seven people. Their suggestions, each based on individual preference and experiences, would undoubtedly send us to wildly different places to carve a claim. Their casual advice could affect our whole lives.

I choose the desk that has rocks and pinecones as paperweights. A woman, stooping over an open drawer, has her back toward me. She turns as I excuse myself. It's hard to make my request and look her in the eye. Instead, I stare at the twinkling of her glasses frames where they are beaded with rhinestones.

"Try the country off the highway before old Valdez. That area is called the Little Switzerland of Alaska."

After joining Richard I want to wave back another thanks at

her, but she's gone to a filing cabinet. It was never her desk at all.

Taking a typed form of instructions on how to walk off and mark boundaries, I fold it into my pocket.

"Let's go now over to E Street, says Richard. "I would really like to leave tomorrow for Valdez. There's no work now, and maybe something will open by the time we get back. Our week at the mission is almost up too."

I follow him outside, adding that our total grubstake is fifteen dollars. The sound of the music is gone. I wanted to march over to purchase our maps keeping step with the brass and drums.

April 29

"Let's just lie down here in the middle of the highway. Look, Richard, maybe it will take this extreme act to produce a ride."

We are on the Valdez turnoff, and there has been no traffic for over two hours. We can't stop walking, though, because of the mosquitoes. They darken the air in their numbers. Both of us have a piece of mosquito netting over our heads. I look into the deep forests on either side of us through wrinkles of mesh. We should have hats with brims to suspend the material a little distance from our eyes. Instead, I only have a scarf, and Richard is in a knitted cap.

We are each carrying the top of a branch too. These we swish above us to discourage the bugs from landing on the net and buzzing by our ears. Yet, it's exhausting. Regularly I have to change hands for the labor. It has been a revelation on the wonders of the horse's tail. It is flicked in barnyards with a great range of assault on any congregating flies.

For the first hour and a half we sang old camp songs and the few hymns that we have learned. Then, we were buoyant. I saw the highway as the yellow brick road leading to our Emerald City. Now, it is an endurance treadmill that we are compelled to walk.

We can hear the motor of the car before seeing it. It's such a necessity that it stop, I want to run out in the road. Realizing we look more menacing than desperate we throw our branches to the side and tear off the shroud of net. We can see an old Chevrolet, and we wave with both hands.

The passengers are an Indian family, who don't even pull slightly to the side, but brake in the middle of the highway. They know there's no traffic to inconvenience. Four small children crowd over in the backseat to accommodate us and our bulky packs. When asked where they are going, the driver only replies, "Ahead a piece." The silence of these people duplicates the dark quiet of the woods.

Slowing the car, the father turns up a rough embankment. It's not a natural break in the forest but one created by a tractor and chain saw. As he stops the motor, his wife gathers a package from near her feet. I can see a log cabin up the rise with a couple walking toward us waving a greeting.

We are observers of neighbors presenting silver-scaled fish to neighbors. The gift smells like old water and is quickly wrapped up again. The insects force us all to move. The men walk toward some machinery parked by a shed while the children chase each other over stumps.

I follow the women. Jean, holding the fish out from her in one hand, tells how she and her husband came from Idaho three winters ago to take the maximum of 120 acres. I notice her calculation of time isn't expressed in "years" but by the sum of their winters.

"It has been a lot more difficult than we anticipated."

Her comment on hardship wasn't really spoken to me, or Alice, the Indian woman. It was a kind of sigh that came out with words, like yawning and saying one's tired.

She leads us up to the screened door of her cabin, then steps back to enter last. My eyes blink in adjusting to the darkness of the interior. It is one square room with a very few small windows. There are kerosene lights on wall brackets. The corner double bed has its covers casually pulled up to the pillows. The walls are studded with nails holding miscellaneous tools, guns, and even parts of chains. There's little place made for beauty. The only decoration is a gaudy wall hanging of costumed dogs, seated around a table playing cards.

I tell them that we have come from Oregon to claim land in the vicinity of Valdez.

"Idaho and Oregon," says Alice, nodding.

The way she pronounces the states makes me ask if she has ever traveled. It's the first time I've seen her smile. She replies that she has joined her husband twice on trips to Anchorage, but didn't like it at all.

The voices of the men draw us back outside. Alice invites us to continue with them; they will drive us to where a second road merges onto this highway. We'll then have twice the chance for a lift.

While yet in the car, and again while unloading our gear, we thank them for going out of their way. The second road is but an empty gravel track.

We strip limbs this time from a small tree. Vigorously I rotate the branch over my head, tapping each shoulder in the motion that confers knighthood. I'll use the mesh when I've exhausted myself.

There's nothing to do but walk and refuse the thoughts of bears raking the air with extended claws, saliva dripping out of their open mouths. They must be out of their winter dens by now and starving for meat. Neither will I imagine timber wolves encircling us in a snapping pack.

The forest does make noises. Trees crack and birds cry.

"Did you know, Richard, there are no snakes at all in Alaska? I read it in the land office."

Looking at my husband I see a cloud of insects above his head and know there's a like cluster floating around me.

The mesh, now in place, makes me sweat. I long to know the time so my complaint can match the number of hours we have been vigorously walking. I would really like to eat the food from our packs, and lie still.

I can hear water. There must be a creek somewhere to the side of us. The bugs can't be dodged but turn with us into the bush. The water is cold and clean from the breakup of winter snow. We follow it looking for the best depth for immersing our canteen. Richard sees the fish. There's a number of dead ones being stored in the water. Too big to be naturally here, a handmade ring of rocks encircles them. They have the same silver look as the ones that Alice handed to the homesteaders.

Richard jerks himself up so quickly from bending over that I feel a spark of fear. An Indian boy in his late teens is staring at us. We greet him and admire the trout.

While I remove the mesh from my face, he tells us, "These are from the river. Let me show you. My brother and I made the trap."

We follow him into the woods on a footpath that skirts a distant cabin. It must be picturesque in the snow, when all the auto parts and pieces of machinery are covered in a blanket of white. It looks like nothing has been thrown away; it is all stored in piles outside for the chance of future use. There's also a cache, a tiny house built up on poles that is the winter freezer for meat.

After crossing over a primitive plank bridge we can see the river. There are two chicken-wire baskets suspended on a framework of poles, turning in the current that can scoop and chute the catch into a trough. Listening to our guide I can feel his sense that this land, belonging to his grandparents, is the center of the world.

As we turn back, Richard asks if we can put up our tent for the night. The boy nods, but offers for us to unroll our bedrolls in a station wagon. With the windows rolled up, we could be completely free of insects.

The car has no wheels and is propped up on cement blocks. With all the seats down we have ample room to stretch out. I wage a small war to annihilate the bugs that have entered the car with us.

Waking frequently, I looked out on a long dusk, then sunrise. This view of an unending evening is the one thread that stitches together all my squares of colored dreams.

April 30

"He did say there are cars!"

Richard and I have made our way back along the path quoting the boy. Once down the creek embankment, we are almost at the road. I refuse to believe that yesterday was a kind of cookie cutter that's going to duplicate itself as today's experience. Looking down the highway I see the distant perspective becoming as narrow as the point of a pin among the trees.

"You know, Laurel, gas here is almost a dollar a gallon; in Portland the top price was thirty-five cents."

"I saw bananas for eighty-nine cents a pound. Back at House of Rainbows they were never more than a dime."

We have had this conversation before, examining other differences in cost between Alaska and the lower states. The conclusion we have always made is missing. Neither of us cites the Alaska wage that will compensate by being much higher.

The jeep affects us like parade soldiers seeing the national flag. We are immediately at attention and raise our thumbs with the flourish of a full salute. The driver wavers. We can see the brake lights flicker with indecision as he passes us. We can only stare at the disappearing car when unexpectedly he changes his mind and stops.

"My name is Smith." He laughs. "I'm the only Smith in Valdez. Had some business in the city, and now I'm hurrying home."

Relieved at hearing our destination, Richard reaches over the seat to pull out his packet of maps.

"I know exactly where there are tracts of available land waiting for claims. I could drop you off right there." The driver takes one hand off the steering wheel and taps the folded green maps on my husband's lap.

"Maybe you would rather go into Valdez first. I really think this is the best part of the country."

There is a romance with land. The dense woods thin with the altitude of mountainsides. We see glaciers and spots of clouds caught below us. There are vistas that evoke an emotional response. If I love Alaska, then the homesteading claim is almost like the vows of marriage. We'll each be promising our best to the other. The long haul of work and sacrifice will demand the commitment that makes all unions work.

There are swallows that soar out of cliffs, riding updrafts of wind. Slow, huge moose feed in some of the gullies by the highway. They lift their ponderous heads to regard us as we whiz by in seconds.

We haven't seen the Alaskan islands or the country that borders the open sea. Each area has distinct features, and a personality of the wild, that others have embraced. Even if we had the money to travel and meet these faces of the earth, I have set my heart toward the mountains.

"Laurel, we don't really have enough food to just go out into the miles of where the claims are. Let's go first into town and get what we need to camp there during our search."

I nod in agreement with Richard's plan. With such a speedy morning passage, we'll have plenty of time today to buy supplies and be back out in the available country by afternoon.

We descend through Thompson Pass, and there are views from some streets in Valdez of Prince William Sound in the Gulf of Alaska. The town has more saloons than grocery stores. But, Smith replies to our questions, there is absolutely no work as he drops us near a corner.

We spend everything but a dollar and a half on groceries. Richard takes most of the tins in his pack. Our provisions, if we are careful, can last almost a week. While walking toward the end of town, I notice it's colder here than in the woods, but there are fewer bugs.

An old man in a checkered shirt stops for us. He's chewing tobacco and keeps opening the window of his pickup truck to spit outside.

"Weather is changing again," he crackles.

I look, and there is a new bank of clouds obscuring some of the peaks.

"Lot of land available here because people want the flatter parcels to do all that cultivating that a claim requires."

"We are just interested in the minimum of five acres," says Richard. "That way the size of our garden doesn't ever need to be inspected."

The old man laughs, approving the wilderness sentiment that the less regulation over a citizen the better.

Richard and I are both staring out at the roadside. It seems to be galloping away as we look for possible features that appeal to us. After passing a creek, my husband cries for us to be let out. We want water on our property.

It's almost completely overcast, so fast has been the bundling of the sky into clouds.

"Where are we?" I ask.

Expecting a sure finger to indicate our area on the map, I'm surprised when Richard shrugs his shoulders instead. "I have no idea," he states.

Irritation strikes me like lightning. I feel a flash of bright heat.

"How come you didn't let Smith really pinpoint things? He knows this land and was willing to help us. Even our driver this morning wasn't given the opportunity to be exact. We just jumped out because you wanted to."

Words can burn as anger ignites anger. Richard's face is flushing.

"Shut up," he says. "You always talk too much!"

My husband has never spoken like that to me before. His voice is as strong as a slap. I walk away from him to a fallen log, where I shrug off my pack and sit with my back toward him. I feel completely miserable. There is no view of Little Switzerland in agony. Instead, there is an intense separation from friendliness and hope. Maybe I was wrong to respond the way I did to being lost, but all the lines of logic in me are swamped by my strong emotion.

"Aren't you overreacting?" asks Richard in a softer voice.

"Probably," I reply.

"Let's see, Laurel, if we can figure out exactly where we are on this map."

He walks toward me, and we sit side by side knowing we'll have to walk only a mile at the most to find a location marker.

A single drop of rain hits the page extended between our hands. With haste Richard folds it, and we spring to our feet. I want to pull out my poncho immediately. Our only experience of rainy weather has been the Anchorage deluge.

Dressed in drab green plastic we stride down the road. The drops are still too infrequent to be classified as a sprinkle. The mountains have all been concealed in a foglike cloud. There is no traffic. With such a sense of isolation it's easy to believe the planet is inhabited by less than a hundred people.

Richard sees the marks of a side road and suggests we explore its first bend. There's no evidence that any recent vehicle has been here. Small plants grow on tracks that frequent tires would keep bare. It's not wet enough for there to be mud. I follow Richard along the path until it ends in a clearing with a log cabin.

An acceleration of rain makes us run to the door. It's futile to knock. We know it's vacant, but I have to first ask, "Is anyone here?"

With no answer, Richard tries the knob, and the heavy door swings open. A small, dark room is revealed. The light from the door creates a line of division from the kitchen side, with its wood stove, over to a handmade shelf constructed to hold a double mattress. There's also a unit of bunk beds for what must have been the children in the family. The dirt makes it feel like a past-tense life.

A mouse darts across from the far corner over to the wood box.

"I bet this is an old claim, Laurel, that the people are just holding now for an investment. Or," adds Richard, "They only come for summers from the city."

I haven't moved my eyes from the wood box. Mice are creatures in plural.

"This is much better than our tent," says Richard.

Only because of the weather, I think. There are mists of webs that hang like gauze across the small windows. Beyond the spiders is a view of the rain.

I fight any revulsion by calling on characters of juvenile literature. Charlotte was an excellent spider, and Gus was the mouse who befriended Cinderella. I need their memory from my back files of reading and images stored from watching old movies.

Richard wants to bring the cheer of a fire. There's a single sink with a hand pump instead of faucets. Wanting to wash the table, I crank it vigorously but there's nothing. Just before I quit, a trickle of rusted water spills down to the basin and, with my renewed exertion, produces a clear gush. It seems like the symbol of homesteading. There will be much effort and temptation to abandon the project, but time will bring us through to the refreshment of a healthy way of life.

After I wipe the table's surface, Richard lays out the map, which has perceptibly aged since its purchase four days ago. We read it, sounding aloud some of the Indian names, until retiring.

May 1

Sounds penetrate the muffles of my sleeping bag. As I first suspected, there are mice, and I hear some sheltering crickets whose hind legs saw night songs.

192

Awaken again, I look toward the windows. There are only two, which flank the door, in the whole structure. It's not raining, but neither is it bright with sun.

Once on the road I'm sorry we can't see the towering mountains. Their frozen majesty is still shrouded by clouds. We walk. Richard has the map protruding from his hip pocket. I've pulled out from my diary the official guidelines for describing a claim.

"Now, Richard, listen to this. It says we must tie our descriptions to natural features and mark each corner with a substantial monument like a mound of stones. If possible the land must be taken in rectangular form and the lines follow the north, south, east, and west of a compass, unless one of the boundaries is irregular, like a river or a cliff."

I stop reading to look at Richard. His charge at me yesterday that I talk too much still lurks. There was a definite barb on that sentence that lodged itself in my confidence.

"What else?" says Richard. He can see that I'm holding three full pages of rules.

"We must post in a conspicuous place the fact that we are applying for this land.

"The rest concerns warnings of what is unacceptable. It says all mileposts, road junctions, bridges, and towns often change and should only be utilized to supplement natural features.

"Don't you love that sentence, Richard? Alaska acknowledges that the handiwork of man is feeble and temporary compared to the creation."

I can see by his face that I'm flying away from him in my speech with my own colored wings. We both sigh. Marriage calls for such tolerance. Sometimes, I don't make sense, and he has to put up with that, while I could let myself be lonely because he doesn't follow some of my ideas and images.

Richard kicks a rock, and the simple game is born. My shots veer the most; nor can they go as far.

I wonder why I'm full of analysis right now; I keep looking at the fibers of our relationship. It must be because we are going to our land. Ahead will be a new level of isolation for us.

The work of establishing a claim will be accomplished side by side in intimacy.

We haven't even been looking for a car, and we don't really want a ride. It's advice I covet when I raise my thumb at an approaching Jeep. A middle-aged couple explain they are establishing their own acres on Fish Lake. The man pulls glasses out of his chest pocket to study the map that Richard unfolds.

"Why don't you get in, and we'll drive slowly to find some marker that matches these survey papers."

It would have been much more than a mile's walk, but finally we come upon a white post that provides our exact location. Everything our eye now sees is available.

Cities are full of those who have been caught in monthly payments for avocado green furniture sets. They work at jobs they don't like and stare out windows at neighbors who have the latest automobiles for no money down and easy terms. Somehow, through a million hooks that would have caught our lives we have made it into the country.

We ask to get out by a meadow where there's a stand of poplar trees, whose new leaves seem to be clapping in the wind. Great moments have music. I have speakers within amplifying "BORN FREE," and Woody Guthrie's "THIS LAND IS MADE FOR YOU AND ME." Others might hear symphonies, or even a choir, but my inner ear rejoices with pop and folk.

There is a creek. It may come from a spring. We have dropped our packs and begin to run as much as the rocks and foliage allow. There's no sense of time, or the metes and bounds of surveying. First is discovery, and then the work. It's so exhilarating to imagine we are the first to explore this territory that I know if I were a child of the past I would go on ships looking for new spice routes. If I had the fortune of a 1990 birthdate, I would apply for launches to outer space.

Richard is ahead of me running along the creek. It doesn't matter that we can't see the mountains. Their formations around this plot will be a surprise for later.

My husband shouts back at me to come. He is now out of

sight. We are both in a strip of woods, whose tree roots are nourished by the water.

I see why Richard cried. There is a real waterfall. It's not a giant one that's worthy of becoming an Alaska postcard, yet it has a little more than ten feet of sheer cascade. The sound of it is full of life. I'm sure the sight of it will never fail to revive me in all that lies ahead. In my mind I impose the seasons on the waterfall and try to imagine it in winter turned to fairy castle spires of ice. I even have our children learning how to walk in range of its shower. *"Now, Hannah, watch baby Matthew."*

"Richard, this is perfect. It can be a natural corner for our claim's description."

With the fact of the waterfall, we have to determine if it should be in the back or the front of the land we want. We must walk through the property on either side of it. For us, who only knew suburban yards, five acres is a sizable lot. I don't even mind the inevitable mosquitoes in the keen pleasure of evaluating and marching off a square of the best property to own. While piling the corner rocks, I already know where I want both house and garden. We have staked a parcel that is part meadow, woods, and water.

"You know what I'm thinking, Laurel. That Indian boy said the best cabins are built out of drift logs. They start petrifying as they float. He explained that a chemical process replaces the wood fiber with a silica that comes from the dissolved sand in the water."

"Should we stay here tonight, Richard? We could put our tent where we'll erect our home."

My husband wipes his forehead with the back of his hand.

"We could," he murmurs. "But then again, we have so much work to do, let's start back to Anchorage."

As best I can determine we have a full legal description that we can submit. Our corners are distinct. Torn out diary pages declaring this area is claimed have been secured with rocks at each one.

"If only we had the money," I complain, "to just come back

with the construction materials we need and use both spring and summer to build. Don't you see a lot of windows, Richard, not these little dark boxes that are so prevalent? We could just plug in more wood-burning stoves if the concern is for heat loss. I think beauty is more important than practicality."

"We'll have both," he promises.

Construction is Richard's canvas and paint box, and I admire him for it. Still, I'm reluctant to leave. My impulse is to walk through our land one more time to pat leaves, put my feet in the icy water, and dream of times to come.

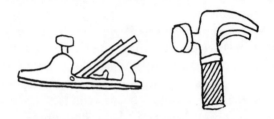

On the highway we mark the entrance to our property with stones. It doesn't seem enough, I would like to blaze an X on a tree. Richard takes my arm as I'm memorizing the configuration of the landscape. He leads me at the pace of a stroll until the entrance gate to our claim is out of sight.

"We'll come every weekend, Laurel, after we get jobs and buy some kind of truck."

Our pace is so slow it's almost a token walking. This way we can turn back if there are no cars within the next two hours.

Because of the steep grade we can hear a vehicle laboring in its ascent. We turn to see a new, blue Volkswagen van. I'm glad at the sight of it just for the hope of a ride, and to escape the pesky whine of insects moving like a line of written E's by my ear.

There are three men, who move over some personal suitcases to make room. They are all pastors riding back to Anchorage after attending a minister's conference. The driver, Reverend

Weeks, extends to us passage back to the city. Richard tells him a little about Glad Tidings and the evangelism of the House of Rainbows. Learning we have only stayed at the city mission, he offers us a room in his church as a place to unroll our bedrolls for the night.

The day has held so much exertion that I begin to be extremely sleepy. Too dull for conversation, I lean against the window glass. There's such a strong potion of exhaustion working upon me that I don't even inventory my desire for a pillow or the other little comforts used to induce sleep.

"You didn't even wake up when we stopped for supper," laughs Richard at my surprise in finding us back in Anchorage.

It is late, and Reverend Weeks has unlocked the door and given Richard instructions for where we can sleep. I follow my husband into the multipurpose room of a suburban Presbyterian church. A preschool uses the facilities by day, and we have to be up and out by eight.

There's a stage, and we pull the curtains across to create a smaller, enclosed area for our night.

ANCHORAGE
May 2

The imposed darkness of sleeping where there are no windows worked against us. Children's voices wake us. School has started a few feet away from where we have been sleeping. The teachers must have a play yard where they wait outside for their pupils to arrive. One voice would have awakened us in time. Instead, the entire student body is marching toward us with a high-pitched chattering.

Richard dashes for his pack to pull out his Levi's. I have to stifle a laugh; I can imagine the curtains being opened and everyone shrieking at the sight of this man in his white, waffle-knit long underwear.

A teacher's voice commands quiet and asks everyone to get a carpet square. I'm racing too, up now and buttoning my own pants.

"Does everyone, boys and girls, want to hear Mrs. Music this morning?"

As voices chorus a sustained yes, I can see the piano behind us. We have seconds to become orderly. There's no time to fold sleeping bags. We pile them into a box at the corner.

One girl screams an accusation that David is poking her. I'm glad for the diversion. We have to think of what we'll need for the day. Our plan is to inquire everywhere for employment. In the past I only checked with restaurants. Today, we must get work. I grab toiletries while young David gets his lecture about what hands are for, and how he should now keep them to him- self. "Doesn't Mrs. Music use her hands to play the piano?"

"And now," says the adult, "what do we do first?"

"Pray," echo the children.

"Help us get out of here," I think.

The supplication on the other side of the curtain is for a good day. "And, 'amen,' to that," I add.

Richard moves our packs to the wall and picks up his shoes. It's so dark it's hard to see anything but shapes. I'm holding both toothbrushes and a comb. Richard pulls me to a fire door that he's discovered. We slip outside just as the curtain begins to open for the magic fingers of "Mrs. Music."

Now safe, we don't even know how far we are from the city center. I'm looking for a gas station before we take a lift. Cars with single passengers appear to be commuters bound for an office.

Once in Anchorage, Richard wants us to meet at 5:00 P.M. in front of the land office so we can hitch back together. He has me copy down the church address, just in case we have to meet much later. I could be hired for a swing shift and be wearing the pink dress of a Dunkin Donuts girl when we are supposed to meet. We part, both infused with hope.

My exuberance begins to wane as I'm told in stores that they are not taking applications right now. I'm losing the heights of my morning's expectations as people shake their head no with false smiles of regret. I, and the cause of our homestead, am worthy of work, yet the refusals are constant.

I walk to the very edge of the city where I catch views of Cook Inlet, an immense body of water that is supposed to be comparable in size to the state of Rhode Island.

I turn back to seek the library; I know the Dewey decimal system by heart. I could sort, dust, and repair bent bindings. It would be wonderful to work with books instead of in one of the many fur shops where I inquired to be a sales clerk. Books have always been to me like a kind of embalmed mind. The dead may be scattered, and who can find them, but their voices live in the library.

Sent to inquire of the head librarian seated by the encyclopedias, I walk the length of the room endorsing myself for confidence. I can quote and recommend to patrons the best in fiction and philosophy. I know the cabbages and kings of literature. I can stamp two-week due dates on the books going out and collect the right fines at the returns post.

"We just have a full staff, Miss, and are not hiring at present. Check back with us about every seven months."

There's no air left in me now. I'm defeated and hungry, but won't spend the fifty cents Richard passed to me when we parted. I vow never to give ear to that slick pronouncement made over vagrants, that they could get cleaned up and get a job if they wanted one. I just hope Richard has found something. It's almost five o'clock, and I haven't seen him on the street in my weaving in and out of businesses.

I find my husband leaning against the wall. People are streaming out the office doors beside him, and his immobility makes him look like the seller of a hot watch just waiting for the right customer.

"Nothing," he says, speaking out the word even before I reach his side. We talk no further, other than my echo of his experience. We move to take advantage of traffic that will be moving to the northern suburb.

The church door has been left open with a note that Reverend Weeks will drop by later this evening to see us.

I go first to Richard's pack to get a large tin of pork and beans. We have bakery bread, too. Richard bought a whole loaf with coffee for his lunch.

There's a kitchen, and I use the can opener from a drawer. I keep comparing our day's search to a game of musical chairs. Even though the melody has stopped, and we are racing for a seat in the work force, we can't find the one that has been vacated. Someone is getting there first.

"I want to go back to Portland," says Richard, leaning next to me against the cupboard.

"Don't be crazy," I cry. "You're just discouraged because we've had a bad day. Tomorrow—"

He cuts me off, feeling too weary to be exhorted.

"No," he says. "Remember, I tried for days before we left for Valdez, too. The only place that said they sometimes have part-time openings was a car wash."

I fill two plates with food and carry them with utensils out into the large room. All the tables and chairs that are set up are of Lilliputian dimensions. We choose the stage and sit a little distance from each other.

"Laurel, we are completely broke!"

"I still have the fifty cents."

Richard sneers, "We are broke. We can't live between the charity of the Salvation Army mission and this church. At least, I can always get a job in Portland, and we have friends."

"We can't quit, Richard. Everyone has stories of how they just held on a little bit longer, and it worked out."

"Sure," he says, "in storybooks. If we ration the food we've bought, we can make it back down into the States as long as we can get good rides."

"Stop this, Richard. We just need some creativity. I went in so many tourist shops and looked at this junk they are able to sell.

We could catch the biggest mosquitoes, encase them in a drop of resin, and sell them as lapel pins or earrings. I tell you, I saw moose scat necklaces for twelve dollars!"

"Come on, Laurel, you're not being realistic! Why don't you get mad at God, not me. He could have opened anything today, but he didn't."

Putting down my unfinished plate, I stand up, too disturbed to keep eating. Almost everything that Richard has said has some muscle of logic to it. Our argument is like an Indian arm wrestle from two points of view. Yet, questioning why God hasn't given us what we need to accomplish our claim pins my hand to the mat.

All through this whole argument, never have I believed that we might go back, until now.

Walking away from my husband, I survey the back wall of the nursery. Every student's name is printed in thick, black letters. Above the official enrollment list are clusters of drawings duplicated from a coloring book on a copying machine.

It fits how I feel. Nothing is the right shade. Wild colors cross each other, and every stroke extends way beyond the lines.

"I won't accept this, Richard!" I know I'm shouting, and I don't care. "How can you come so close to your dream, as we did yesterday, and even think about walking away?"

"I had a lot of time today to really consider things, Laurel. Sure, I tried as hard as I could for work, and prayed that something would open. I can only deduce that we are to do something else than put our lives under a bushel basket."

I hate him appropriating a scripture that puts Jesus on his side. It is manipulative and unfair.

I keep walking around the room thinking that though I was disappointed by the day, it was nothing but a small ditch. I'm in a chasm now and still falling, as all my plans are being wrenched from me. There is no comfort.

I look back at Richard, who is sitting still, feet dangling over the edge of the stage, with his eyes averted. He has used such soft words for the hardest of arguments. He's made no move to silence me, but only wants to convince me to change my mind. I don't even want to be around him, nor do I want to go into the sanctuary. By calling our claim a "bushel basket," he's arrayed the whole Sermon on the Mount against me.

Without a word, I walk outside, not knowing where I'm going or when I'll be back.

The early evening light is etching the mountains quartz pink. I feel separate from their beauty and at a great distance from the order of all the homes I'm passing.

Something about Richard seems wrong, too, even beyond his dinner-time decision. It's his abruptness and his propensity for changing course. He declares we'll sell the house, buy a kilo— go and stay, like a weather vane that is always ready to blow around in another direction.

The sea of my rage is receding, but in its place is a mire of self-pity. I keep walking to find the right place to be alone. It doesn't take long to find a swatch of raw country. I climb over some fallen tree trunks a tractor pushed together in a heap at the end of the development. I sit, and behind me the city sprays insecticide, while before me is a dense and tangled wood.

I cry until I'm exhausted. There are so many graves in a life where countless hopes must be buried. It's as if my sorrow is in plural, now understanding the suffering of what other lives have known.

Now, all those pictures of what living here could be belong to a younger woman than I am. The idea of Alaska first motivated me and then sustained me through every difficulty. My dream of a cabin is now lifeless. I so wanted to tack moose horns above our door and put a giant thermometer on a window ledge. I'll never see the waterfall again, or ever know the contour of the mountains by our land. There were babies to be born here, and I even had chosen their names.

I feel I've lost Richard too; at least I've lost the way I used to perceive him. He's no longer that luminous star set on a straight course. There are other magnetic fields that pull him. I can't just close my eyes and fly with him without checking the atmosphere for myself.

Gingerly I touch my eyelids. They are sore and swollen. My back aches from hunching over, and I slide off the log onto the dirt, where my shoulders can lean against the wood.

I can feel a difference within me. My monologue that alternates complaints with despair is really a form of prayer. I'm not talking to myself.

Spreading out my hand I look down at my wedding ring below the wrinkles of my knuckle. There's a tracing of dirt too, in some of my nails from establishing the corners of our claim. Everything is gone, but God.

I just don't feel like responding with the solid gold yes, of a right attitude. "I'm your daughter, at duty. Put a dove on my shoulder. May I make the angels smile." I'm too distraught to be willing and obedient.

Yet, there's nowhere else to go. I can feel myself surrendering to the fact that God has a plan for me, for us.

I can accept now returning to House of Rainbows. In being available to meet needs, it's promised that mine will also be met.

Richard is not at the church when I get back. I'm glad, because I still don't feel like talking.

I wonder if we climb to heaven over the ruins of many cherished schemes.

Richard has pulled out both of our sleeping bags. Mine has a note pinned to the top. Reverend Weeks came to get us to spend the weekend with his family. He will be back later, my husband writes, and tomorrow we can go to the Weeks's house.

We will sleep with the curtain open tonight. I am at peace with my decision, but wonder if I would stay in Alaska if allowed.

I hear Richard come in. I want to let him know that I'm his partner again, but I'm too tired to extend the gesture.

May 6

The pitted windshield, outside the arc of wipers, is full of bugs. Richard and I are both up front on the bench seat of the van next to Reverend Weeks.

The weather is warmer today than what we have known before. Motioning for Richard to crack the window, I appreciate that the pastor is giving us a lift to the junction toward the Yukon. Our packs, in the trunk, are full of washed and folded clothes.

"This is the only highway east. I'm sure you'll get a ride straight through to Canada."

We thank him as he pulls to the highway shoulder. Our two-word phrase of gratitude has to cover the details of how they unfolded their living-room couch and welcomed us. Their daughters, also, lent me shoes and a dress for the Sunday service.

"Oh, one last thing," says Reverend Weeks, "my wife packed some food that you can use today."

Taking the lunch from his hands, I can feel the weight of fruit at the bottom. Curious to know the contents of our sack, I'm hoping they have included some cellophane-wrapped desserts. Once we are alone I open it.

No one could miss the envelope that stretches across the entire bag. Exclaiming that they have given us something, I pull the envelope out into the light and tear it across the top.

It is cash. There are four twenty dollar bills, a ten and a five. Richard whistles in surprise but makes no move to fold it into the safety of his wallet.

"I never hinted that we were broke," says Richard, "and I know you didn't either!"

My husband takes the fan of bills from me and smooths them into one roll. He taps my arm with it as if he were an English gentleman touching me playfully with a glove.

"Tell me what you would do Laurel, if I said, let's go instead to Valdez and try to work there. This could stake us while we look for jobs. It's only early spring."

I look at Richard to see if he is teasing. I can read nothing in his smile except that he really would go if I say yes.

Having looked at the money, and his face, I lift up my eyes to the low ridge of hills.

"No, we are to go back to Oregon. I am certain of it now." What I feel for Karen, Jack, Leon, and the rest, known and unknown, will be the real land for investing our substance.

Richard severs two branches to make fly swatter "tails." There are lots of bugs hatching in the small pools I can see across these flats. This water, created with the thaw, will evaporate through the summer. I survey the landscape, feeling that Alaska was one of the last toys of my childhood. I did want it with the passion of a face pressed against a window glass.

"Would you really go to Valdez now, Richard?"

He has no time to answer. A battered car pulls to the roadside. A man with shoulder-length hair gestures to us. He has removed his backseat from his vehicle to enlarge his space for hauling supplies. There are garden tools and a scruffy dog that springs up from a scrap of throw rug.

"That's Jake. He's part timber wolf."

The dog does have yellow eyes, but I still doubt the lineage.

"I can only take you about eight miles; that's where I turn toward my claim. I've taken five mind-blowing acres. Hey, you guys look cool. Open the glove box."

Richard reaches for the knob. Inside is a large plastic bag of marijuana.

"You must use a lot of oregano," I say, feigning innocence. "Are you Italian?"

"I grow it," he boasts. "Not on my land, but in a secluded place that still doesn't belong to anyone. When I can get it, I fertilize it with bear dung. There's some papers there if you want to roll a few joints. Hey, take a pinch for the road."

I let Richard's be the voice that declines.

"Have you ever been to the Haight?"

I confirm that I once lived in the Haight-Ashbury. It was only eleven months ago, but it feels more like a decade.

"Are they into crystals there?" Our driver pulls out of his pocket a small piece of rose quartz.

"I never go anywhere without it. You know, it's thousands of years old and full of the energy of the earth. It releases vibrations that give me direction."

"Have you ever considered the Bible to be the source of instruction?"

He laughs at us for the last mile before turning off onto two tire ruts that cross a meadow.

"No," says Richard, having held on to my question of Valdez. "I don't want to stay here."

We walk, him slowing his pace and me quickening mine so we can stay in step. Richard kicks a rock, and lacking aim I knock it into the ditch.

Finding the next stone, I'm edging it out with the side of my boot when a truck with Texas license plates and a simple plywood camper shell pulls to the roadside. Completely gray, the vehicle's color seems to have been created from pouring together all the cans of garage-stored paint.

The driver climbing out from the cab has a flat top cut so short it shows his scalp.

"You-all are welcome to ride back here. There's a mattress, but we do put our son back on it for naps."

I can see a three-year-old in a T-shirt solemnly regarding us out the back window.

"We're going to Canada, and just want to get through that territory of dirt roads lickity split." With a punctuating laugh, he unfastens the back doors.

It seems that about an hour has passed when we stop, and the blur of the passing wilderness re-forms into a view of trees. Our container is dark, with only small windows that have chicken wire embedded in the plates of glass.

"This is Joshua. It won't take him long to fall asleep." The child crawls toward us equipped with a yellow tin truck and a picture book. He has a drawl identical to his father's as he demands that I read. When he denies that he is even an itty bit tired, I suspect it's his parents who need the rest.

The third time through recounting the travail of a little steam shovel that couldn't find his mother, I'm corrected for abridging the script. The child has memorized it, and insists I be faithful to the paragraphs. He rehearses for both of us all the noises machines can make and the cries of both domestic and wild beasts. Without pause, the boy wants to know how high I can count, but doesn't wait for my reply. Joshua announces he has conquered math up to the triple digit and starts his recitation.

At "twenty-nine, thirty, thirty-one," Richard sighs and stares at me as if this is all my fault.

In the fifties the child begins to pick his nose, but no itch can deter him from his goal. As he nears one hundred, I feign sleep.

It's my hope that by removing Joshua's audience, I might get him to grow still, but his voice never hesitates.

Stretching out by me, Richard whispers that we'll remain with our hosts only through the Yukon, then disembark when the road is paved again.

May 11

Lying next to my husband, I turn to survey our rearrangement of the truck interior to give us more room. We have stacked the two spare tires on top of each other and secured the center cavity with the driver's case of black-eyed peas and some automotive tools. Richard is asleep. I'm listening to the droning sound of the motor and the rush of vehicles passing us in the opposite direction. Traffic is increasing, which gives me hope that we'll soon be in Dawson Creek.

I've pulled the curtains on the window shut. They're just rectangles of cheap cloth strung on a wire. The shafts of light were at such an angle that I could watch galaxies of boiling dust. It was at first entertaining, something to look at other than the dull interior. I pretended that my eyes had a microscope implant that let me see the invisible. But once I began to consider that I'm breathing this stuff, I had to erase it awhile from my view.

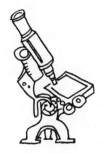

I expected to spend these last five days in private mourning at leaving Alaska. Instead, I've been using the same old mechanisms that aided me in my past when I fell out of love. I concentrate on every flaw, while during romance I emphasize every quality. I've given calculated consideration to the number of bugs on the last frontier. The first mosquitoes of the season are the largest ones, which lived through the winter by hiding in the bark of trees beneath the moss. As the summer progresses they always get smaller, and bite harder. There are also "no-see-ums" and flies. They are ferocious enough even to drive the caribou up the glacier slopes to escape. I'm really glad to go.

Hearing pavement beneath us, I pull back the curtain. There are some small houses. I wake Richard. We must be at Dawson Creek. Rising onto his side, he blocks my view of the window but confirms we are in the outskirts of town. I pull down the tires to see out the other porthole.

Our host pulls up the cement apron into a gas station. My joints ache in the minutes it takes for him to instruct the attendant and walk to the back. I have to move. I've suppressed until now the full thought of how uncomfortable this ride has been. I have the urge to shout, "Let us out"; I can barely refrain from pounding the door.

We both squint in the flood of light and instinctively block our eyes with our hands. Our time in the interior was like life in sunglasses. We lived in a box under the sea. Richard doesn't bother to inventory what we've spent at the little one-room stores and cafés along the highway. He wants a real bed and bath too.

From rechecking the record of my diary, I see it has only been one month and four days since we departed from this town to go north. I can feel the ghost of my old self walking down the main street seeing the same shops and window displays. Yet I feel ancient by comparison with that eager girl. It was as if every twenty-four hours added a year to my subjective age.

"Let's just go back to the same hotel," says Richard while taking my arm to cross near the mile 0 post. Near the curb I read aloud the No Vacancy sign that is leaning against the window glass. In addition there is a notice tacked to the door that says Sorry.

We turn to look for another accommodation, choosing to walk south—tomorrow's direction out of town.

The lobby of the North Star Hotel is full of artificial plants. I imagine it must be meant to be an oasis during the winter's snow. I find it suffocating, as if the plants remove oxygen, photosynthesis in reverse. There's a monotony to all these identical green leaves. They are dusty, and I rub an imitation pink petal and eye a plastic bird as Richard rings a buzzer for information.

"It will be seven dollars for the two of you," says a woman who puts her head out from a back door.

We know some of the hotels in Dawson have accommodations for five dollars, but we're too weary to bother. We don't even check the room first; we just pay, and Richard takes the key.

Following my husband, I can see there's wallpaper through the open door. It looks like the print of a fat lady's dress from 1950. The colored, crossing ferns could have been made up into leisure wear for a Hawaiian cruise. I even imagine I see random sweat stains.

"What are you thinking?" asks Richard, who is walking all around me to open the small closet and drawers. By contrast, I haven't moved since I stepped over the threshold.

"An enormous lady perspiring while doing the hula in our wallpaper." Ignoring my nonsense, my husband asks if I want the first bath.

"I bet, Laurel, there's two tubs, and I won't have to wait. Then, we'll put in a load of laundry and go eat."

Dumping out my clothes, I'm dismayed that everything is again dirty. I don't want one shirt to miss the wash. If only Richard weren't so adamant about appearances, I would drape myself in the top sheet like a sari until my denim skirt was dry. If he's concerned what his wife looks like, I could cover my whole self, like a friendly Halloween apparition, and peer out of the cigarette burns for basic navigation.

Richard is long gone with his hotel towel while I'm still looking for my shampoo. I'm glad my husband has taken the razor so I have an excuse not to shave my legs. We've clashed in the past because my idea of beauty is being natural, while he prefers a denuded calf and thigh. I've told him, "You can take the girl out of Berkeley, but you can't take Berkeley out of the girl," but he doesn't understand.

"No, that is absolutely crazy! You can't wear blankets and towels to a Laundromat!"

We are both standing back in the room. He has been dressed for some time, and anxious to go, while I've just come in with a towel around my hair and the cotton sheet knotted in a sarong.

"Okay," he says. "I'll do the laundry myself!"

I hoot back in a delight of acceptance and, once alone, sleep in the middle of the bed.

As we walk down a side street to look for a promising café, I can tell that Richard thinks I'm getting out of hand. He decides on the restaurant with a tone of muscle-flexing authority. I'm sure he's asserting himself as a backlash from doing the laundry. He regards it as woman's work.

We go into the one place that still has some tinfoil Christmas decorations on a back wall. The juke box has a flashing lighted panel. There are more men than women, and no children at all. Yet I do see two high chairs pushed together in a corner.

The menus feel like a thousand fingerprints have been pressed onto the laminated plastic. We both want the special, set off in a double-outline rectangle: a chicken and fries dinner.

"I hated doing the wash," says Richard. "Never again." We are waiting for our food, and both of us are feeling irritable.

"They don't tell you anything at the Laundromat. There're no signs, nothing."

Richard explains that he put in too many little boxes of the soap that is dispensed from a vending machine, and suds began to ooze out onto the floor after he opened the door to check it.

"Some small children started playing in it, and the mothers were glaring at me!"

I exaggerate to myself the sight he describes by thinking of bubbles up to the customer's knees and foaming out across the sidewalk. We may be almost broke from Richard's investment in soap.

The salads are put before us. Richard's complaints end as he lifts his fork to eat.

"I bet once we get back to House of Rainbows it will be like we never left at all. Our whole trip north then will be like our private parenthesis."

"Probably," replies Richard. "What we need first is a trip to rest from this trip." I have to laugh, but I know Richard is not joking. Maybe it's a good thing we have so little money, because I'm sure my husband would want to drift until it was gone.

Abandoning my fork, I pick up a drumstick with my fingers. I'm remembering that he decided we would leave Portland when the church offered him the opportunity to train as a printer. It was the moment that really accelerated our departure.

I look over at Richard, who is dabbing his lips with a napkin. I think my husband sees responsibilities to be like different-sized bales dropping from the sky. I bet he figures they can't land on a moving target.

"Now, where would you go?"

Richard replies with the word, "Well," as if I have handed him the Golden Catalog of Journeys and we can wish for anything.

"We've never crossed America together, from the Pacific to the Atlantic coast, or seen Europe. What I would really like to do, Laurel, is hitch to Florida and get a job on a boat going to ports around South America."

His words do affect me. They make my own wings itch to unfurl and fly in the winds. I'm no better than my husband. We are both candidates for never-never land. I remember it's the second star to the right, and Peter Pan took the boys there who never wanted to grow up.

Silent now, we finish everything on our plates, including the basket of cellophane-wrapped crackers. We have developed the mentality that the Lees are about to starve, and we have to fortify ourselves at every chance.

I look around the restaurant at the people in booths and seated along the counter. I'm so aware how much most people's lives need an additional dose of adventure. Take a spoonful from the tonic of mountaintops and desert scapes. Our deficiency is different. We require a daily vitamin whose ingredients include church and work. I know if it's prescribed for a long time it might be hard to swallow.

I take Richard's arm, and we stroll back to the hotel. Immediately sleepy, I want the bed to act like a wand that will quickly turn my thoughts to dreams.

May 14

Realtor's cars are all alike. They are big, American-made, and have plush seat covers. It's almost as if they simulate the comfort of the very living rooms they hope to sell to the customer beside them. I'm letting Richard sit up front and pay the ticket for these miles by listening to our driver's small talk.

This Chrysler has such good shocks that my pen doesn't waiver as much as it does in other cars. Some of these diary pages look like a secret code, or words penned by the oldest hand alive. Skimming my recent entries, I can also see the number of restaurant stops that I've noted in the margin. We have been treating ourselves, as if a hamburger or a hotel bed is a kind of compensation for turning back.

I'm not even sure of the distance to Vancouver. I've let myself be lost in the vast highway system of Canada; at our departure I monitored every milepost.

"This land over here has been bought for a shopping center. I sold it to a developer from Los Angeles, and I'll be renting out the shop spaces myself."

Pushing a button the driver lowers the window into the panel of his door. All that I can see are trees lush with summer leaves in a field.

"I'll probably need a second office. Lots of opportunities here for young people who want to settle in this area and raise their families." His eyes seek out mine in the rearview mirror.

Instantly depressed, I feel the realtor's words touch something within me; it was his reference to raising a family.

I know I want children. The thought of them began in Alaska, and I'm still carrying the idea of a baby Hannah first, then her brother, Matthew. There are recurring impressions of a warm, tiny head leaning next to my cheek.

"Now, here's my card. You just never know if you'll need it. Or keep it in your wallet for someone else."

Our driver, the eternal salesman, has pulled off the highway in an area where there are blocks of ranch-style homes amid the farmland.

Richard adjusts his pack and then holds up mine so I can slip it on. There's a moderate flow of traffic and ample pull-off space so we can walk while still signaling for a ride.

"Do you want children, Richard?"

His answer is the same as it was during courtship, when we were exploring the past and present of each other. The issue was discussed along with questioning each other's choice of music, politics, and pizza toppings.

"Well, of course, but not for a long time."

It's the voice that means the minimum of a decade.

My silence makes him declare, "We're not ready for that yet! Everything's all right, isn't it, Laurel?"

I nod yes unable to torment him by waiting the seconds that would create panic. Richard actually sighs in relief.

We have momentarily forgotten about hitchhiking, although our thumbs are still on duty. A Volkswagen van pulls to the shoulder in front of us, its bumper swaddled in layers of stickers. The middle door slides open, and as I step up into the interior, I can see a number of people lounging on a mattress. Because of a pile of visible packs, I guess that most of the passengers are hitchhikers.

Richard adjusts a guitar case to make more room for our gear. There's a smell of incense and pictures of Indian gurus stuck along the visor with playing cards.

The boy next to me is too young yet to have a beard. He is wearing a turkey wishbone at his neck tied onto a leather thong. The driver introduces himself as an organizer of rock 'n' roll dances who manages a number of bands and operates a strobe light show. The vehicle is going to Vancouver, and there's an open invitation to spend the night at a commune operated by the parents of the boy whose neck is decorated with the turkey bone. Richard neither commits us nor refuses with a declaration that we must continue south.

"You see, there's nothing in a cupboard until you open it, or nothing around the corner until you turn it."

The speaker is a bearded man seated up front with the driver.

I'm ready to refute his prevalent philosophy, but no one is listening to him anyway. Long-distance apathy has made every mind dull. Time is just being endured.

I settle back, resting my head on my hand with my feet curled up to give Richard more room.

"Take this exit, and turn to the left."

Every one stirs. Those who are sleeping stretch and wake up. Wishbone is up on his knees leaning over to instruct the driver.

We are in a neighborhood of older homes. It's easy to tell the owners from the renters by how the yards are kept. The house, the object of our guide's gestures, is an old Victorian. Present-day occupants have trimmed some of the wooden frames of the windows in bright purple paint. There are also distinct violet smudges where drips were wiped but never erased. Numerous dogs are on the front porch and in depressions across the lawn. At once they rise to stare at the vehicle pulling to the curb.

Hoisting his pack over one arm, Wishbone tells us his real name is Gentle Thunder. There had been no real introductions in the van at all. He seems both proud and embarrassed by such a title.

It's unlike Richard to include us with this party of chemical astronauts each now sorting out gear. Obviously, everyone here has taken many flights to the faraway places of inner space. I have expected an announcement that we are broke again to come at any time. Our participation in this offer of hospitality confirms for me our economic status.

A naked child of five opens the door, calling out that "Gent" is here with his friends. She loves her brother and grabs his leg and wants to ride on his foot down the hall.

"This is Snowflake," says Gent to us, but his eyes stay focused ahead looking for his family.

The parents, both with ponytails, merge into the hall to greet Gentle Thunder and screen his guests. Introducing themselves as John and Edith, they know more about narcotics police and their disguises than their sixteen-year-old son does.

217

The questions to us all are friendly, but we have no further entrance into the home until everyone supplies a statement of where they have come from or where they are going. They trust their own radar of intuitive senses.

Special status is conferred on the driver, and on us as a couple. I'm sure it is the Alaska homesteading account that wins for us the offer of the couch in the living room that unfolds into a double bed. The other passengers are instructed to put their bedrolls in the basement. Snowflake offers to lead the way and show off her box of kittens, which can't open their eyes yet, living under the stairs.

Gentle, with his parents, takes the driver upstairs. The father wants to talk the language of rock bands and asks for news about The Great Pumpkin and Georgia Straight.

Momentarily alone, Richard and I seek the living room and find it provokes the feeling of entering a kind of clubhouse. Four bicycles hang by their back tires from hooks inserted in the ceiling. Various traffic signs are hung at random.

Three young men sit around a table. They have torn the want ads into pages that are being held up in front of them like a peculiar game using giant cards. Engrossed in their activity, they barely acknowledge our entrance. Listening to them each read aloud, it is obvious by their accents that they are all Americans. Their age makes it likely that they are draft dodgers now seeking employment across the border.

Most of the window coverings in the room are Canadian flags, giving the house the appearance of being an official sanctuary for those who want to avoid a call to Vietnam.

Richard piles the cushions to the side and unfolds the couch. Neither of us are tired, but we want to claim our territory in the midst of an unknown number of residents who might also vie for this bed.

"I'm sorry," Richard whispers to me. I know he's referring to our depleted finances and this night's accommodations. There's such sincerity in his voice that I let the balm of it cover other issues.

I walk to the window. The flag isn't wide enough to cover the glass. Looking out, I can see that the porch light has attracted a number of bugs to orbit around the bulb. It's the first time in a month that I have seen the moon against a dark sky.

May 15

From Vancouver to the border stations is the only stretch of highway that we have never seen. Looking out the windows of the van I realize we don't need the ferries this time to circumvent what is now our right to go home.

Richard is angry with me. I could see the dark clouds beginning to gather at the breakfast table, and then his thunder eyes glared at me.

I couldn't stop talking through and beyond our morning's meal. Edith, the mother of the house, and I discovered how much the other likes to read. Ignoring first the oatmeal, then those who were bringing their gear to the door, we kept exchanging titles, quotations, and characters. We moved faster than proper sentences. Lightning struck when Richard grabbed my arm and insisted that it was time to leave.

I've only got a few more minutes before we are dropped off, and I'll have no umbrella for his storm. The flags at the border station are just visible now, and the lines of cars waiting for clearance are beginning to form. We both thank our driver, who is going to turn around with the others and take a Canadian highway to the east.

I look at my husband's profile as he pointedly ignores me by staring straight ahead.

"You'll be better off if you don't say anything," mutters Richard in his stern voice. He quickens his pace to be slightly faster than my own. He has not looked at me once, and all that I can see now is his ramrod straight back.

I'm angered by the censure of both his voice and his body language.

"I wouldn't mind at all if you found someone to discuss topics you enjoy."

When he makes no response, I become immediately sarcastic. "There are the wonders of construction, Richard. That's a subject you can't have any meaningful dialogue on with me."

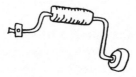

There is no acknowledgment that I have even spoken. His ignoring of me makes me escalate now to rage. I chant, "Composite roof, four-inch nails."

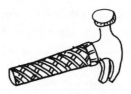

I don't care who hears me or what I look like. I shout at his back, "Phillips screwdriver!"

I succeed in getting Richard's attention. My husband spins around and grabs my wrist. His face looks blotched with squares of red and purple. My emotions distort us into a piece of clashing modern art. My head is a tiny white triangle.

"Do you have anything else you want to say?"

I shake my head no and start to cry. I'm aware that we are providing a real diversion for motorists, who have little else to watch but red brake lights in front of them. Glancing down the line of cars, I can see we are the object of everyone's attention. Wishing for privacy, I start walking next to Richard. On foot we can now move faster than the vehicles. I wait until I'm far ahead of those who first witnessed us before I wipe my eyes. We'll make a new line of front-row seats for our drama.

"You just sounded so crazy," says Richard. "You and that woman made no sense at all. For over an hour you kept it up, and people were waiting to go."

I feel the stinging pleasure of wanting to sob without restraining my volume. I need the release that's possible in noisy sorrow, not constricted sighs.

I remember Edith quoting Jane Eyre, "that to talk to Edward Rochester after ten years of marriage was like an animated and audible thinking, so suited are our minds and character."

There's no anger now, just a keen loneliness. The words magnify something that I feel is wrong between us. We lack compatibility in the area of exchanging ideas.

Everything else feels difficult too. We have absolutely no money. With good rides, we could get to Portland and the House of Rainbows, but our bedroom there is sure to be occupied. We'll have to hang sheets in the basement to create privacy. Our trip is over, and we have little to look forward to.

My mind feels full of invaders that pierce me. Every thought has the barb of a spear point.

Richard reaches over and takes my hand. "Come on, Laurel, we are almost up to the inspection office. Pull yourself together, and let's just get through this."

Wiping my face with the back of my free hand, I let Richard pull me toward the building behind the Canadian flag.

The attendant listens to Richard answer, "Aberdeen, South Dakota," as his city of birth, and I add, "Chicago," as mine. As he's about to dismiss us Richard inquires about highway regulations for hauling a prefabricated log cabin north.

"A time is coming that we might just come up and buy some land. There's a lot of beautiful, open country."

I clench my fist until my fingernails indent my palm. I've got to do something to get control of myself. I can't believe Richard's question—as if he might decide someday that we should try it all again! I'm so weary of living in circles, and a little afraid of what I might say to my husband once we are alone. Our relationship is more fragile than I ever before believed. I can feel lots of sharp fingernail words that would tear us apart.

Overflowing with emotion, and knowing there's not one thought that can be an ally, I start repeating one phrase to myself: *"Help me, Lord Jesus."* Word follows word without pause like a line of bricks building a wall. I won't let any other images through.

We walk the few hundred yards to the U.S. office. Our feet crunch the gravel, and the sound of it blends with my repetitive plea. Sometimes I enlarge the word *"HELP."*

The American agent wears a government-issue khaki brown shirt. He only wants to know if we are transporting fruit or any kind of plants into Washington. I can hear the boredom in his voice from having to ask the same question to an assembly line of travelers.

Richard seems lighthearted at being back in the States. Starting to hitchhike, he even pumps his extended hand. There's a steady stream of cars just beginning to escalate to highway speed.

"I wonder," he says with a short chuckle, "if we'll still find Leon at House of Rainbows."

The name provokes my memory of him and Cliff always slipping in the kitchen to go down the basement stairs. It was the only place where they could consume their packs of cigarettes. Our room is going to smell like an old bus station. We will have to sleep in a cellar with intermittent clouds of smoke. I retreat back behind my wall of prayer. This time I magnify the word "LORD."

A green van pulls to the shoulder behind us. We look back to see if it's for us or if they have stopped to merely consult a map. The driver taps the horn as invitation. Unlike our other Volkswagen carriers this one has no bumper stickers, and the rear seat is intact. Both men, in their early twenties, are real college boys in button-down collars. They have been traveling for a few weeks across Canada and just want to get home. I sense they are mere imitations, not real free spirits.

"I live in San Francisco," says the driver, "and Mark here lives in Boston. Where are you heading?"

Richard answers Portland for tonight.

I withdraw from the conversation until it's almost just a sound and give my attention to the wild daisies that blur with our speed to clouds of white. There are flowering clumps of foxgloves, too, that provide a contrasting pink.

My eyes need to swallow beauty as if it's a peculiar tranquilizer. All these capsules of color are poured along the hillside for consumption. The higher the dose, the better I'll feel.

"That would be wonderful. Don't you think so, Laurel?" I turn in apology for not listening.

"They have asked us if we will drop them at the SeaTac airport and deliver this van to San Francisco."

"Look," says our driver, "I just need to get there as soon as possible." Mark, sitting next to him, adds that he wants to get back east, and they have been looking for the right people, people who seem trustworthy.

Richard wants to know if we can be allowed to take five days for delivery as we have friends to see in Portland. Also, he requests gas money. The driver voices agreement with his terms.

I look at my husband in respect for his negotiating ability and study the car interior with appreciation that this could be our rescue wagon. The airport is south of Seattle, and first it must be determined what flights are available before we can be released with the keys.

Walking with everyone into the terminal, I tell myself that they are going to change their minds. It's an "almost" story. I don't want to ride hope up like an escalator only to have the machinery stop. The fall would be terrible.

And what about San Francisco, I argue with myself. We'll only have to turn around and hitchhike back to Portland.

I study the display boards of departures. It looks as though all of America is one flight away. I can feel the planet shrinking to distances measured by hours. It's such a contrast to hitchhiking, where time is subject to thousands of variables and oceans can never be crossed. The world seems a giant place to me.

I have never learned our benefactor's name. He and Mark buy tickets and hand Richard a twenty-dollar bill. They return to the van for their luggage, and one draws a detailed map of exactly where to deliver the vehicle.

Richard, now at the wheel, drives them from the parking lot to the sidewalk entrances of their carriers. Once alone, we try the horn and the windshield wipers.

"In two hours we can be in Portland," declares Richard.

"No," I reply. "Let's savor this and go camp somewhere. We need to be alone tonight, and we can go to the House of Rainbows first thing in the morning."

There're lots of woods with dense, shady places where we can park. Tomorrow I'll have the strength to see Karen, Jack, and the others to exchange our stories and look at the basement.

Richard takes a freeway exit. He is always ready to meander. I'm thinking in fragments of a psalm; there are pastures, and still waters, and words about my soul being restored.

PORTLAND
May 16

I don't know why I expected the old house to stay the same. At our departure I must have photographed it with my mind and put it in a kind of time warp. We get to go away and change, but I didn't want the House of Rainbows to alter in any dramatic way.

We park across the street from it as if we need the extra distance for observation before making an entry. The porch has become a catchall for things. Karen and I talked of finding clay pots and planting flowers, but now cardboard cartons flank the door. Even from here I can read the instruction FREE written across the box and see clothing remnants spilling over the top. There are bowls on the stairs too, that must be used as containers for pet food. From the beginning Richard had maintained a policy of allowing no personal pets at all.

My husband takes the time to lock our Volkswagen's doors. We cross the street together. It must be about ten in the morning, and Portland's weather feels unseasonably hot. One of the neighbors has used an extension cord so a television set can be operated on a porch. The sound of it dominates the neighborhood.

Near the stairs we can read the number of signs that have been posted to the wood siding for the purpose of endorsing God and salvation.

"Now why didn't they just go to a junkyard and get a couple of free car bumpers for all those stickers,"comments Richard. He is showing good humor in the face of an obviously different management.

The door is not locked. Someone has tacked the Bible verse "Knock and it shall be opened" by the handle. Following Richard in, I feel all the curiosity of a visitor and am now stripped of the familiarity that I once knew as a resident.

Karen and Marcie, seated on the floor with a number of women, spring to their feet upon seeing us. I can almost hear the sound of sheep as we're being embraced. The "Welcomes" have a distinct bleat in the chorus of voices.

Richard separates himself, hearing that Jack and Eric have been in the basement all morning with some others. I want to ask why they are there and push the question in with hundreds of others that still have to wait until Karen finishes her Bible study.

Once I've sat down I notice that most of the women are slightly bent over a small square of cloth that they are embroidering. The floss, needles, and scissors are on the rug, which explains their peculiar huddled configuration. Accessible tools means no one has to interrupt the teaching to ask for something to be passed.

I can tell in the flash of Karen's eyes crossing mine that she is as eager to go away and talk as I am. There's a slight sigh that she has the morning duty of the lesson and still has to tie all the strings of ideas together into a final bow.

"The globe is full of religious paths that are posted as the way to God. Some have nice names, and travelers call back for people to follow them. But, Jesus Christ," states Karen with hands that have suddenly become alive, "is the only way."

The needles around me never stop piercing the fabric and pulling the thread through the pores of the material. There are squares of sunlight on the floor, and swatches of rainbows are refracted through the beveled glass. There's something that looks other worldly about this setting that a Dutch master could duplicate in oils.

"Don't be deceived," concludes Karen. "No one can come to the Father, but through the Son, and he's the Messiah."

The women rise, and what was a painting changes to a dance. Motion of rising and stretching surrounds me.

"Come on, Laurel, let's skip lunch and take that time for a walk. You know it's just another day of peanut butter sandwiches."

Only someone who eats regularly can so glibly talk about forgetting a meal, but still I agree. There's usually a surplus of loaves of bread branded with a black X to denote its day-old status.

With the television still blaring, we automatically turn to walk in the opposite direction. Enough people have cut across the lawn to thin the grass into the beginning of a trail.

"The house is bursting with residents now," says Karen. "Some of the brothers have even cut out a hole in the ceiling and constructed a ladder to use the attic."

Karen pushes her long, blonde hair back behind her ears. "The basement is holding the church's new printing press. Eric was sent to a typesetting class by Pastor Peters to learn how to operate it. We are making our own tracts down there to pass out on street corners."

In her rush of comments one of my questions receives its answer and disappears. The opportunity of training for the job of a printer has long passed from Richard to another.

"Who's in our old room?" I ask.

"It has become an additional girl's dorm," replies Karen while opening and shutting her fingers to indicate numbers passing through. One woman who stayed in there brought her bowl of goldfish to the house and would sign up for the bath only to use it to 'exercise' her fish.

"Oh, Laurel, so many crazies for God have been through here! One guy wanted to set up a bench downstairs and manufacture crosses with batteries that operate tiny flashing lights from all their corners. Someday, he insisted, they could be wired for sound to play hymns, and by wearing them, one would be a real witness of faith!"

I laugh with her but sadness lurks in my heart. There are so many who come out as Christians but are not at all, and by their preposterous conduct they sully the reputations of those who are true.

"You know, Laurel, we can't even fit in all the members. Leroy, with a group of other men, are out in a camp planting trees, and there is no space available for their return."

As Karen talks, my assumption that we would return from San Francisco to be residents is fading from a Technicolor idea to transparency. Her continuing descriptions allow no substance for that plan. Besides the lack of room, I'm reminded of absurdities. Brother Carp once insisted that we pray over bits of cloth and sleep with them under our pillows. He told us they were to be used for healing, so I laughed and took it for my personal handkerchief. I really don't want all that again.

"We'll be getting our own house as soon as Jack and I get married. We want to live by the church, and we've been saving money for rent."

The sun is on her upturned face, and I can see almost microscopic small white hairs above her upper lip. Karen goes on to elaborate that she's embroidering the yoke of her muslin wedding dress for an outdoor marriage celebration. A potluck will help cover the expense of refreshments.

While she talks I can almost see her plans as animated. Dancing Disney figures surround Karen Anderson. Dreams have such happy faces and abundant energy.

Looking away I remember that my own ideas about our homesteading were like a cartoon troop of bobbing moose horns.

"We want to get a Volkswagen van too, like the one you are delivering."

Karen is listing plans for me now with the speed of a woman checking her shopping list. She's speaking about buying a van as if it is as easy to pick up as a head of lettuce.

It's so clear that my experiences provide a more mature perspective. I'll look forward to conversing with her after some months of real married life. By contrast, I know nothing more about our future than that we'll be leaving in the morning to deliver the car to an address crumpled in the back of Richard's wallet. By then we'll be broke again and in a city.

"Jack and I both love antiques. I want that look in my house with homemade braided rugs."

I feel I have two choices, to faint in uncertainty, or to trust for another rope to be lowered from the sky for Richard and me as we let go of the one now in our hands.

"What do you want to do?" asks Karen, almost apologetic that she's been talking so much.

We're standing along a flower bed that has been cultivated between the sidewalk and curb. Someone has pushed a plastic marker into the earth to tell us that the specific variety of iris next to us is Purple Fantasy. The word sparks an answer.

"Find a little place of our own to live and decorate it with my own kind of art. We need a church too."

I'm still not ready to tell the Hannah and Matthew portion of what I want for tomorrow. I'm sure that the birth of children will provoke other conversations ahead, and a seasoned mother would be amused at my innocence.

We have no shadow walking back to the house; the sun's in its noon position. The men are out on the porch when we return. Jack jumps down the three steps to greet Karen, while Richard chides me for missing lunch.

Once inside I walk through the rooms by myself. There seems to be an invisible sheet of Plexiglass covering everything. I can see through it, but there's no entrance for us anywhere.

PORTLAND
May 17

Richard has what I call "sleep breathing." It's a slow, but rhythmic, propulsion. Even with my eyes closed I can hear him ascend through the layers of sleep. I know exactly when to talk and not be charged with the complaint of waking him. I will use my soft, rustling sheet voice, and my words can overlie his last and fading dream.

We have spent the night in the Volkswagen van in front of House of Rainbows. The backseats convert to a bed, and the closed curtains are now acting like a net to catch the first of the sun's rays. The material is a plaid, cut from the bolt of an India import gauze. I have been watching the blue and purple begin to glow with morning.

"Richard," I whisper. "Let's take our time getting to San Francisco. We can travel slowly along the coast highway."

Rolling from my side to my back, I stare at the white vinyl ceiling. I want days of a view of the sea, wildflowers, rocks breaking the water into foam. I'm dreading the inevitable search for work, and now I want to delay its realities. I keep remembering all those eyes in Anchorage that looked into mine while refusing me any chance of employment. I will see that face again.

We'll have no money for food, not to even mention rent. We can't live with the people I know in the Haight-Ashbury because of all the drugs; nor could we ever move in with my parents. That only leaves one alternative: another Salvation Army rescue mission.

Richard rises up on his elbow. I can see the sparse shading of hair on his chest.

"I don't get it," he says, "Why do you use the crack of dawn to suggest we don't hurry to California?"

I laugh, and express relief that the city can't possibly get us with its bony fingers today.

"Okay, Laurel. We can go part of the way on the coast, but I want to get to Frisco early so we'll have at least a day to use this car while we look for work."

We go quietly into the house to wash and collect a bag of food allocated for us last night. After shutting the refrigerator door I see the week's list of chores and the rotation of house members who will do them. Whoever assigned the people to their categories substituted a Bible person for the real names. The translation key is at the bottom, but it looks as though the apostle Paul will be cooking breakfast with Moses and Queen Esther. There's no looking back from the porch this time. The season for us to be here has finished.

Even though it's early, I slide back every window, filling the car with cross drafts. Maybe it's the sound of the wind, and Richard's whistling, that encourages me to try and stick to this moment. Tomorrow will take care of itself. I've got to stop picturing us gathering information from vagrants: "Where are the soup kitchens and temporary shelters?" I picture my denim skirt as a mass of fraying patches.

Out the window are scarred mountains known as the Tillamook Burn from an earlier forest fire. It's Smokey the Bear's landscape for testifying against carelessness with matches. The floor is again green with floral and bush cover, but the black stump trees stretch for miles.

Coming into Tillamook, we see the familiar pastures filled

with herds of dairy cattle. Traffic increases as we near the town center. All the parking lots adjoining stores are also filled. Richard comments at the crowds.

"What's happening?" I ask a pedestrian crossing in front of us. A daughter is tugging his one arm while he fields the traffic, not being at an intersection.

"It's the Tillamook Day parade!"

We can't afford the dollar being asked by one man waving a pennant to advertise his front lawn as a place to put cars. We turn around to seek the outer periphery for leaving our vehicle.

I can hear bands, and the impulse to run shoots a kind of electric current through me.

"Come on, Laurel, will you wait up?"

I look back at my husband. He's wearing his old army shirt whose fabric is permanently indented where the field badges were removed before resale. Smiling broadly, Richard shows his whole row of upper teeth, which accentuates the tan he got hitchhiking across Canada.

I'm going to just pretend that this van that will be waiting for us is ours. I am Cinderella going to a kind of parade ball. Midnight has not yet struck. When the Volkswagen disappears, we'll be back to rags and menial work. My prince, almost up with me now, is a pauper.

The crowds ahead define for us the route, then as we approach, we can see the exhibits themselves. There's a large pickup truck with little girls from a local dancing class standing in a cardboard cage doing the twist. Their mothers used a week's worth of makeup on those lips and cheeks.

Following them is an old man riding a bicycle that is pulling a wagon filled with logs. There is a sign on each side advertising Hinkerson's Home-chopped Fireplace Burners.

A little girl with the name Mary inscribed on a card around her neck is pushing two lambs in a baby buggy. The spokes are entwined with streamers of colored crepe paper.

I drop Richard's hand when I see the Tillamook cheese truck coming around the corner. There's such activity, I know they are throwing samples into the crowd. The gift turns out to be a white tissue paper hat, but the forest ranger slings tiny, wrapped candies from his window. Some children have paper cups full, but I'm only able to retrieve a couple of red-and-white peppermints.

I'm entranced by the local enterprise, and San Francisco with its hardships is now feeling even farther away. I think to myself:

FORGET IT ALL, STAND TALL, SUMMER'S COMING

CALIFORNIA
May 19

"What are you thinking?" asks Richard.

I'm at the far corner of the Volkswagen's bench seat, and I have to admit that I have been unusually quiet. My mood has confined my speech to single syllables since we crossed the California border. Now, we have merged with the Bay Area traffic on the freeway. Richard has already heard duplicated lists of my fears, so it just seems better to shrug a reply of "Nothing."

The truth is, I've been imagining the kind of hourglass that is usually associated with New Year's. I can feel the sand pouring through what little time we have left with the advantage of this car. Today we'll arrive, and tomorrow the van must be returned to San Francisco. Personal landmarks are rushing by me as I recognize by both buildings and signs that we are almost there.

"Richard, let me show you Berkeley. It's where I lived and went to school. It can all be done in an hour."

As he agrees I point out the University Avenue freeway exit. My tour for my husband feels like my last-ditch effort before walking into enemy fire. The bullets are notched with the questions, Where can we work? and Where will we sleep?

Driving up toward the campus I point out the largest of the health food groceries and an art shop where I used to occasionally buy a print. A million ghosts of my old self are provoked to life by the sights out my window.

I want to park so that we can walk through the eucalyptus grove and the glen where Strawberry Creek runs across campus.

For us a parking place has to have a prepaid time left on the meter. Richard agrees to a slow cruise to look for a vacancy with a black arrow that marks some remaining minutes. He runs down Telegraph Avenue, and I'm doubtful that the main road that accesses the center of campus will have a space. The activity of the meter maids here is especially ferocious. They have tiny vehicles like a motorized shark's fin, and we can't risk a red violation tag, which draws them like blood in the water. I'm disappointed, and the memories are singing louder and louder.

On my side is the Bank of America, which used to have enormous windows, but they were broken so often during the student riots that they were replaced with a permanent brick front my last semester.

"There's one!" cries Richard. I whip around to look where he's pointing and am amazed to see a full forty-minute scholarship for the streets.

In every direction is something of interest that I would like to show my husband. Tugging on his arm to go left toward the campus, I remember Holy Hubert at the intersection shouting for God through his missing front teeth.

Richard pulls harder, and the opposite way. He sees a drug

paraphernalia shop displaying an array of colored and flavored cigarette papers. The number of street vendors has doubled. I've already walked by batches of handmade earrings that look as elaborate as sports store fishing lures.

Richard is almost crowing at the drug-age window displays. Just as in the Haight, there are piles of oregano to simulate marijuana. The record shop has a giant papier-mâché joint with a mechanism that ejects clouds of bubbles into the street. It draws a number of lighter-than-air spectators to enjoy the film of flowing colors. I watch the students too, with book bags flung over their shoulders. They ride by on bicycles, or pass us on the sidewalk as we look into the storefront windows.

It all brings the time systems of the academic semesters back to me. As a member of the class of 1967 I should be getting my first degree. The thought does produce a sigh, but I can't let myself drift down the path of "What if I made a choice for a wider classroom this year."

Catching up with Richard, I point out that my former street is right ahead, a block away from Telegraph.

At my old corner is the one face I recognize. It's Blind Bob at his post requesting spare change by the grocery door. Peering past him into the interior, I remember buying my very first yogurt out of its dairy case. I never worried then about having enough money for food. My line of poverty was drawn in clothing stores, not over loaves of bread.

Now, I'm curious to see the old building itself at the corner of Haste and Dana. It's my turn to insist on our direction. It becomes quieter as we turn the corner. Out loud I estimate we have about twenty minutes left on the meter.

I never noticed before that there are two churches at the other corners of the intersection. In my selective perception, I looked for interesting men, not houses of religion.

"Think, Richard, that just a year ago this was my home. In June I made that brief trip north searching for enlightenment, when I met you."

The building that I'm pointing to is a three-story box with the land under it becoming more valuable than the rental units. I study it while remembering the studio I shared with Arlene. We had bunk beds at one end, a lot of art reproductions of Tahiti at the turn of the century, and a kitchen the size of a closet. Tom lived next door and had a growing collection of soft drink bottles that eventually covered his floor.

I can't help but go in the vestibule. The rug looks like the carpeting from a movie theater with its repetitive, gaudy pattern. It's worn through to the boards by the door and up the stairs. I'm amazed that the soda pop machine in the lobby has the same Out of Order sign.

I find it disorienting that everything is so unchanged. Even the very smell and sounds from the street reinforce an illusion that I've gone back in time.

"Well, if it isn't Laurel Moore!"

The pronunciation of my maiden name startles me. It's as if it confirms that there has never been a husband, or a year of wandering. I am again the girl, and student, who wants to get her master's degree in social work and marry a professor.

Turning to find out who has spoken, I see Richard first still standing in the doorway. The sight of him puts my internal compass aright. Pivoting now to the voice behind me, I cry, "Why it's Gideon Raz!"

"Richard, this man and his wife managed the apartment building."

Gideon nods that this is still his employment while insisting we come in and greet Nadia, and see his new daughter.

I explain that it will have to be brief because of our ticking parking meter, while flashing four fingers at Richard to signal the minutes we can allocate for a visit.

I remember that Gideon is a graduate student from Israel. This is the first time I've been invited beyond the doorway, even though I used to come once a month to pay the rent.

Their interior has a feeling of the Middle East. There are three trains of wood-carved camels arranged on table tops. Nadia comes out of the kitchen, puts down a can of poppy seed paste, and wipes her hands. She's a plump, dark-haired woman, a contrast to her freckled, fairer husband.

She asks if we'll stay for coffee. As I refuse, Richard accepts. The smell of it is in the air. Once the men have taken a sip from their mugs, Nadia leads me back to her bedroom, where a crib has been pushed diagonally against the corner.

The tiniest baby, like a little mound of flowered flannel, is in the corner. She looks like she's sleeping on both her tummy and knees. Almost bald, the baby has hair not even as long as a nap of velvet. It's more like a shoe polish head that promises to be brown like her mother's. There's such a strong smell of powder that vapors must ascend with each diaper changing to make a layer in the atmosphere.

While watching the mother smooth the cotton blanket, I'm pierced with the desire for a child. It's such a strong yearning that I want to get out of the room so the emotion can subside and become extinct.

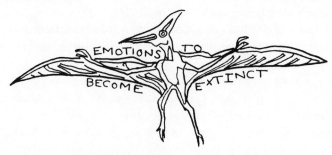

Richard is talking to Gideon about the house he had been planning to build if we had stayed in Alaska. I ask for a dime, glad to escape with the excuse of the meter.

I carry the coin, not trusting it to my pocket. Walking to the apartment door, I have to listen to my husband describe the waterfall on our land claim.

Once in the lobby I can run, and as I bolt toward Telegraph, the memories come crowding back. I was always sprinting from my apartment to every lab and lecture. Then, I wanted a bicycle, and all I had to do was go to my parents' house and get it.

It's easy to cry as I weave among the pedestrians. My past is a strong ghost telling me that everything was once better; the future has almost no voice at all.

I just want my tears to defy gravity and fall up. Can't they each be a prayer, and every sigh be a petition too?

At the van I find we have five minutes left. I can't even climb into the privacy of the front seat, because I didn't think to ask for the keys. Already motorists are beginning to slow down in hope of a vacancy at the curb.

There's something comforting in looking into the meter and watching the point rotate to the side for more time.

I stroll back, and drying off from my emotions, begin to count the number of men wearing beads and to notice that none of the women I pass are wearing nylons.

Richard is standing up when I come back into the apartment. I'm glad that he is ready to leave, as now there is time to show him a little of the campus. But I see it's excitement, not the fact of departure, that has brought him to his feet.

"Laurel, Gideon has offered me a job. A lot of apartments need both cleaning and painting. He'll exchange our labor for free rent, plus a salary."

I want to sit after hearing the news, but the men are going up to see the available unit. I follow them upstairs, and suddenly they are not moving fast enough for me.

On the third floor we go to the very corner where I lived one floor below. It's the identical studio, but filled with clothes and bits of things that were abandoned. There are about thirty dead plants in pots.

"The renter left this bed," says Gideon, "and I have a storage shed you can check in the morning for more furniture."

The kitchen is dirty. Dishes were left in the sink, rather than washed. There's a cockroach on the cupboard. I see some canned goods pushed to the back of the shelf. Richard leaves with Gideon asking for instructions where to park the van for the night.

Once alone I start running the water until it's hot. There's even a container of liquid detergent under the sink. I open the window before I start to clean, and I can hear the sound of singing from the street.

My mind, in gratitude, is full of pictures of people bowing. Some flex their knees, bend their backs and drop their heads. But for me, I feel like lying prostrate—we've been rescued again.

BERKELEY
May 21

I'm waiting for Richard. He's gone either to get the combination to the storage shed lock or bring back Gideon so we can get inside. I can't wait to see what we can use from the collection of abandoned furniture. He should have already returned, so I can only assume he has entered the "Coffee Zone" of visiting the Raz apartment.

Leaning back against the storage shelter wall, I consider going after him. It's so easy for me to act like a wooden spoon that stirs the batter of my husband. Maybe I'm so anxious to get inside that this feeling is more like a motor on an electric beater that wants to whip the word *hurry* into Richard.

I easily title each five-minute increment. Gideon and Richard must be now Talking Business. This apartment building is just one of the properties owned by the Gong brothers, who have an office somewhere on Shattuck. They are even building a restaurant in San Francisco.

I slide my back down until my knees buckle and I have to sit in the grass. Its luxuriant growth has escaped the blades of a lawn mower and the path-making power of repetitive feet. It smells like childhood fields where I built forts and never wore shoes.

I can feel changes coming. We already have a house and food. I'm about to get furniture. Everything is ahead. There will be an auto with a baby seat and a new Sears barbecue grill sticking out of the trunk. The children are quarreling again over who gets to sit by the window. I'm driving Hannah and all her boxes away to college, and Matthew, still in high school, is so tall that I have to readjust the front seat after he has borrowed my car.

It's all here in the smell of summer in the grass, and the waiting. I feel I'm touching one of the links that intersects time.

The back apartment door slams, and an overweight girl carrying a cat walks toward Telegraph. She's followed by a student with a book bag who crosses the parking lot to a sports car. I think Richard has forgotten his quest and might have left with Gideon to Review Damages and Estimates.

Springing to my feet, I feel an urgency to find him. This is supposed to be my moment of compensation, when I get to collect instead of disburse. Everything that I've had to give away is about to bounce back to me.

"Come on, Richard. All that I need is the lock's combination numbers."

It's as if my thought is a cue hissed behind the curtains, because out steps my husband with Gideon. I say nothing but a syllable of greeting. As a young nag I'm silenced by an observer.

Gideon has the numbers written in his wallet. As he twists the dials I have a flash of wild hope that there will be some antiques inside with every leg carved like an animal's foot.

From the open door wafts a smell from childhood of my grandfather's potting shed, a room full of black shapes.

"I haven't really looked in here myself," says Gideon. "We

just took the apartment with the furniture as it was left by the last manager. I've put some boxes and things here inside the door in case anyone came back to claim something."

Gideon's disclosure brings mystery to the room, a feeling that this is an unexplored tomb full of Berkeley's artifacts. We are archaeologists. I'll be the first to analyze the fragments of pottery to see if they are representational of the plastic age by being dishwasher safe.

"Oh man," hoots Richard. "This place could be full of dope!"

My eyes keep pushing through the shadows. With each blink I can see better. There are piles of furniture. It's obvious that at one time the apartment units offered the option of coming furnished. All that's visible are modern-issue couches and chairs with thin legs that unscrew at the top. It must have come from the same factory that furnishes cheap motels.

At the side are piles of large blue glass water bottles.

"Oh, Richard, let's take those. Our bathroom is so long, narrow, and sterile. We can place them along two walls in a solid line of color. We'll put fish in some, and plants that will trail out in others."

"I'm not carrying all that weight to the top floor!"

Richard's voice is final and heavy. I had simply overlooked the problem of their transportation.

Out of Gideon's boxes, which ring the door, we find our personal treasures. I like handmade mugs even without handles. There are several tie-dyed T-shirts, which once washed will be great for summer. Richard opens an antique tin for plug slice smoking tobacco. It is empty, and we add it to our new pile of goods.

I can carry everything in one load up the stairs while Richard labors behind me with one water bottle. I'll use it as a vase, as its mouth can hold one flowering branch.

As I put the stuff on our table I ask him why he made me wait so long. There's neither anger nor accusation in my voice. Time takes away that, but not curiosity.

"Well," replies Richard. "You didn't have to sit there and

could have come over yourself to the manager's apartment."

I don't know how to explain to Richard that I'm avoiding for a while eye contact with Baby Girl Raz.

"Anyway," continues Richard, "we were talking about me joining the construction crew on weekends that's building this Ponderosa steak house in the city."

I cross over to sit on the bed. It's such a small room that no one can go beyond conversational distance. Not having any bedding yet, we have our unzipped sleeping bags covering the mattress.

"Why, Richard?" We need to find a church right away that's something like Glad Tidings."

"Look," he says, "this is the best opportunity we have ever had to get ahead. We need everything, and I would be a fool to pass it by."

I feel irritated by his all-or-nothing attitude. We can measure our work with both play and devotion.

"Just take Sundays off."

Richard interrupts any further paragraph from me.

"Of course," he says, "I will in time. Laurel, we've got to get our front teeth back in. You know we'll even be able to afford a car, and lots of other things we have always done without."

I say nothing more, hoping he's right. We have exchanged so few words in all these internal thrusts of his hopes and my fears.

Richard invites me to go down to Telegraph and buy some ice cream. He has some advance money from Gideon. I'm glad to go and leave the issues. I know they can't disappear and will probably wait for us right in this room.

BERKELEY
June 8

Midway through wiping the table I stop to look at our savings account book. This time I don't open the cover to run my eye down the growing list of single- and double-digit deposits. The sight of the blue cover is enough. It's on top of the refrigerator where Richard first put it the day we opened an account. I even have my favorite teller, who doesn't smirk even when I pass her a couple of dollars at different visits in one day.

I resume my efforts to remove my hot cheese sandwich crumbs from dinner. Everything seems to take twice as long waiting for my husband. I'm distracted into every tributary. It's already dark, so it must be close to ten. I'm listening and waiting while my hand wipes patterns of scallops and spirals onto the wood. I stack horizontal lines of moisture, remembering Lincoln logs and as a child how a pile of them made a house.

After wrapping the bread in plastic, I store it in the refrigerator to keep it safe from the possibility of a roaming bug. The food has to be rearranged because we are so rich in packages of hamburger and chicken legs. There's the coins of a leftover casserole. Food is another kind of currency. And there again on top is our book of proof that we have over two hundred dollars in savings. All of it is vibrating ever so slightly while the motor churns autumn air for the shelves and winter for the freezer.

All that I'm doing is waiting for Richard. He went with Gideon after he finished painting an apartment and joined the construction crew in the city. I have library books in a stack by the bed so I can dissolve time with stories of space warp travel and aliens invading earth. I checked out *Pilgrim's Progress* too, but it looks like it might be tedious. It's escape I want, not instruction.

I decide to brush my teeth. The mirror on the medicine cabinet was set so high it reflects my chin but not my neck. Foaming lips are at the bottom of my reflection. They seem like another sign, along with my wandering mind, that I'm going mad.

I think of Mrs. Gideon Raz, living flights of stairs below me, who would never consider notching her walls to mark her husband's absence. She doesn't understand my feelings of being stranded in an apartment that's like Robinson Crusoe's deserted island. Instead, a tiny daughter fills her arms and absorbs her time. I can't wait nine months to be busy with a Baby Friday.

I wipe the sink and return the towels to the rack in perfect order. While crossing the room, I straighten a chair and pull two dead leaves from my flowers. Once on the bed, I consider my need for employment. Maybe I should go back to school; then I'll qualify for a real job. With a degree and diligence, I could earn thousands. I wonder then if in twenty years of accumulating profits I would be wiping a Victorian pedestal sink and straightening plush towels. There would be more rooms then to walk through to my bed, but what would it all be for?

I turn to look out the window, as if to turn from the face of my thoughts. Some ideas are unwanted guests, and I don't feel like hearing their peculiar monologues.

244

Outside couples are gliding in the warm night air. My wedding ring keeps me from slipping out the door and into their midst. I could be a young twenty-one laughing aloud in a Telegraph Avenue café.

Hearing Richard's key in the lock, I think of him as rescuing me, rescuing us. I don't know how to hide how desperate I am for his company.

"Did you have a good day?"

We both ask the same thing, like a bookends couple now supporting volumes between them.

"Let's go out, Richard, just for a walk or something."

I can see the refusal winding up in the forehead wrinkles and the way the mouth puckers before pronouncing the word no. He is tired.

I'm going to plead a second time after he comes to sit on the chair. He brings in the smell of smoke with him. I think of fellow construction workers exhaling it like exhaust.

There's something else too. It's a more subtle odor that I can't quite detect. It has an acid tang of old leaves by a garage heaped into a bonfire. It isn't the burnt pumpkin of marijuana, but alcohol.

"Richard, you've been drinking!"

"Oh, what does it matter that I had some wine, and I guess a few beers too. We stopped on the way back, and one of the other guys bought it."

I'm surprised that he thinks that it's the money spent on booze that I'm objecting to.

"You could have insisted on coming home first!"

"Laurel, I'm telling you this is not a big deal."

Feeling stricken, I watch Richard rise to start the water for a bath. Watching him walk away I realize it's not now that I am afraid of; it's knowing that the pattern for tomorrow is in today. I feel that I'm getting a glimpse of how our life will be if we don't make a change.

"Richard, please, let's go outside."

Maybe it's my voice with its stricken tone, or guilt, that makes him concede. Richard turns off the faucet and replies, "Where do you want to go?"

I'm up. Some chances don't last more than minutes. I'm afraid that even by answering him I'll extinguish it, and I have no particular destination in mind.

I imagine that I can smell the beer, with the smoke, out in the hall. I can feel my husband behind me, about to protest. He'll never make it down all those stairs and out to the street. Any moment his desire for a bath and bed will tip the scale, and he'll retreat.

"I've never showed you the roof. I don't think that even Gideon has taken you up here."

The door is unmarked and resembles the others in the hall. Someone removed the Fire Exit sign a long time ago. There are only a few stairs and now the entrance hatch to the roof, which budges with my thrust.

The air outside feels full of currents that have swept through trees and over water, unlike what is so stagnant to breathe indoors. Because of the city lights only the closest stars are visible.

I lead him over to a small structure that makes a back rest.

It was a year ago that I was here last. Ted and I would smoke our marijuana and talk about poetry and enlightenment. I'm sure that beneath my feet are some of my old matchsticks, like tiny bones that have become fossils of my earlier life. The real evolution is only on the inside.

"Laurel, I know this has not been an easy time for you. You are used to us being together, but there's so much opportunity here. If we stick to it, we can make a lot of money within a couple of years.

"I am twenty-eight years old, and it's time for me to put down some roots. It's been good for me too, to be with men who work every day. I've only had two sets of friends before. At House of Rainbows they sat around and read the Bible, and my friends before I met you sat around and smoked dope."

I'm struck by the truth and sincerity of what Richard's saying.

There are no street lights here to illuminate our features. We are gray phantoms speaking to each other. All that I can conjure for a reply is pictures. Strong emotions seem to separate images from words. I am trying hard not to cry, so anything I say will be uttered with a voice that wavers.

"I agree, Richard, that we need roots. We want our life to be like a tree that gives to others fruit and shade, but to grow that way we need certain nutrients in the soil. I've looked on Sundays, while you've been working, but have never found a Bible-teaching church. And we don't have any friends who are believers here. What we know about Christ isn't enough. It has to be pruned and watered. Richard, you can find a job you'll like in Portland. We have enough money now to rent a little house and even buy an old car."

I have to exert myself to stop and maintain a time of silence. Pressure from the momentum of ideas is pushing me, but Richard has turned his head and seems to have locked himself away in the jury of his thoughts. I promise myself not to murmur at his decision.

I look out in the direction of the bay. There's only a dark void in the encircling lights.

It's not our salvation that's at stake, but whether we'll be careless or careful with what we've learned. How does it go—that old parable of the virgins? Five were wise, and five were foolish.

"Okay, Laurel, we'll go if it matters that much to you."

Who knows how we bury song lines and melodies? The right moment opens the hatch door, and out bursts the old words.

247

Leaping up to my feet, I exclaim, "I could dance all night, and then I could dance some more!"

Richard stands up too. He says he is going to get a bath, and I'd better prepare to go with him tomorrow when he talks to Gideon, as he's going to blame everything on me.

Our marriage feels whole again. We are working together toward what really matters. I love and respect my husband.

"You know, Laurel, that baby of theirs is really cute," he adds. "I wanted us to offer to watch her one night so they could go out for dinner or something."

June 15

I'm the one hitchhiking. Richard says it's because I initiated the decision to go back to Portland, but really we both know that it's the smartest configuration for getting lifts. Richard bought before we left a Swiss army knife, and he's sitting in front of our gear carving a little knot of wood. It resembles a doughnut, and he slips it into his pocket when we have to run.

"Come on, Richard, tell me what you're making."

"I can't tell yet. It could always be a paperweight, or maybe a napkin ring." As he speaks he turns it around in his hand. "I should carve on it a map of all the places we have traveled on the West Coast."

His sentence ends with half a sigh. I know, like me, he's remembering all the times we have gone north and south on this highway.

"It's hot enough, Richard, that I could take off these shoes and wear your carving as a piece of jewelry for my toe."

We are full of school yard banter in the leisure of waiting for the next boost north. There's a smell of heat baking both ground and grass. It shimmers over the distant landscape in the kind of wiggling rays that children draw to define the sun.

I have never measured time from January to January as in the custom of calendars. The new year always begins for me in summer. It was those childhood swimming pools that started me comparing my accomplishments one year to the next in the progression from the shallow end to the depths.

Richard asks which bag has our cans of juice. I'm glad to release my arm from its ninety-degree angle of duty and let my rigid thumb relax. It seems there has been nothing but station wagons loaded with gear halfway up the back window.

I stretch out next to him as he finds the right attachment on his knife to pierce a drinking hole on the top of our apple juice.

"We sure know this part of the road!"

My husband makes the statement not expecting a reply. It's uttered like a yawn.

"Please, Richard, don't think of our year as going around in circles."

Putting my hand on his leg, I can feel that some of the day's heat has been absorbed into the fabric of his new jeans. I wonder if I can put into words my picture of time being like a spiral. What we love, and learn, changes the dimensions so we can be a little higher with each repeating curve. But it feels too hot to utter ideas of any destiny. All our talk this morning is sleeveless.

I stand to resume my post as a human Yield sign. I should dress in bright yellow with pocket flaps that I can pull out to caricature the standard diamond form.

"It feels like we're stuck here," says Richard, bored with his whittling.

"Well, if we have to settle on this bank, we could tell time by the blackberry bramble. Look at those branches in the gully. The berry is a tiny green knot for June. I wonder if there will still be some red leaves left to mark November."

My monologue is interrupted by a string of cars. Vehicles seem like social animals that have to travel in packs. I won't talk now. In this moment of their passing flash I want to present myself as serious about getting us a lift. We do need to keep going ahead.

Epilogue

The Lees did rent a house in Portland, Oregon, that Laurel described in her diary as surrounded by blackberry bushes. Richard obtained full-time employment as a school bus driver, and eventually they bought a small home walking distance from a church.

Laurel continued writing and illustrating diaries through the years while caring for their three children: Matthew, Anna, and Mary Elisabeth.